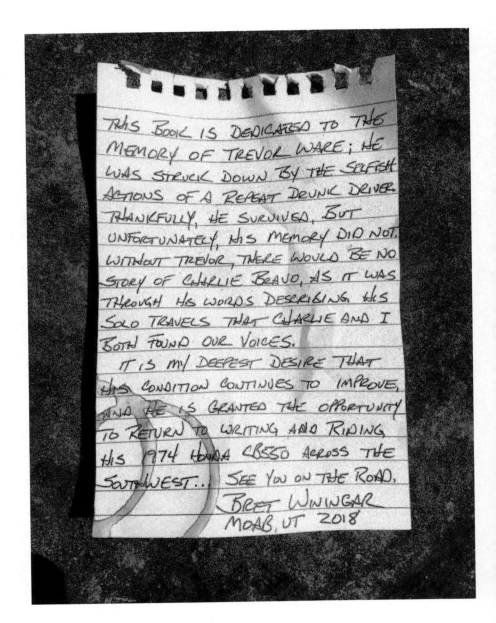

Un millon de gracias...

To Zach, for the ride of my life.

To Hannah and Tania, for starting the Facebook page

To Theba and Joey the Garden Cat, for the boost and momentum

To Uncle Larry, for giving Charlie her voice

To Nathan and Chris, for the steadfast support and advice

To Fletch, Craig, Kyle, and every other rider to twist a throttle with Charlie

To Gary G, for his always incredible artwork, vast knowledge, and belief in the message

To Gary D, for his inexhaustible devotion to the cause; without his expertise and guidance, Charlie and I would probably be carving hieroglyphics into stone instead of "mass communicatin'"

To Mom, for her forbearance and understanding during those countless times when I stayed too long in bed with the dogs piled on top of me while Charlie struggled with a post, as well as those times that the inexplicable call to go "vacilando" was too strong to ignore. Without Mom, there would be no Casa del Whackos; there is not another like her, on this planet or any other.

To you, the followers of Charlie's story from around the globe; your kind words, deeds, and most importantly, your continued support of the message that we all matter and have a contribution to make is the high-octane fuel that keeps this engine running

And most importantly, to Him from which all things originate.

Twas ragged and raw and the riders saw

She had been there for quite a while

In a crate in a field with no end in sight,

No houses for many a mile.

They stopped for a bit, then left in a cloud

Of dust and exhaust so blue;

She resigned herself that this was her fate–

The crate was all she knew

She pricked up her ears as a sound approached and the riders came back into sight.

So weak she was, she could barely move,

Her famine overcoming her fright.

But here was a change, hands reaching out,

inflicting something much different than pain.

They left once again, came back with a truck,

And headed for home in the rain.

Due to her plight, she spent the first night

Sleeping with Zach and the bikes.

Hondas and Harleys, though great on the road,

We're not the bedpartners she likes.

Next day at the spa with Alex and Ma;

Transformation taking place all the while.

First the smell, then the pain, vanished down the drain

Leaving a black coat and white smile.

As her confidence grew, her message did, too

That we all live in some sort of crate

But no matter how hopeless our conditions may seem,

Hope never fails if we wait.

Now she hogs dad's whole bed, from the foot to the head

She's the Queen of the Casa, you know.

She rides on the back, of a Honda so black

Her name is Charlie Bravo!

Charlie: And so it begins...

I can barely remember a time that didn't involve the hard plastic interior of this crate. Sure, faint memories of a little girl's birthday party with the expected squeals of delight when I was presented remain, but it was only a short time before the "cute" wore off and was replaced by the reality of caring for a rambunctious puppy.

In today's electronic world, many things vie for a child's attention, and unfortunately, in the competition between a living creature and the latest smartphone app, I lost. I found myself being confined to the crate with increasing frequency, first for short periods, then as my owner's conscience began to sear over, for longer sentences, until soon I wasn't let out at all. My infrequent meals consisted of a handful of dry kibble occasionally tossed into the floor of my prison, only to mix with my own feces that had begun to fill the confined space as well.

In spite of such meager rations, I continued to grow, as did my frustration and claustrophobia. The arch of my spine was the first to suffer, followed by my hips, knees, even my tail, rubbed completely through to the bone from the constant contact with the interior of the crate. My toenails also continued their relentless growth, eventually curling back under and growing back into the pads of my feet. I learned to sleep in my own filth, curling my forepaws under my chest to conform to my tiny area, but during the day, I would occupy myself by gnawing frenziedly at the inside of my plastic cell in an effort to free myself.

Eventually, the combination of crying, scratching, and the stench from inside the box became too much for even the foul mistress of the house, and on a cold night in January, I felt my crate being hoisted into the back seat of a creaky small sedan smelling of stale cigarette butts and desperation. Even at that, the hum of the four-cylinder engine and the warmth of the heater lulled me to sleep until suddenly I felt the car veer off of the pavement and onto marshy earth.

The rear door was yanked open and the dome light illuminated a small weedy area. Before I could think to protest, the crate was slid from the back seat to land with a squishy thud on the soggy ground, then footsteps retreating hurriedly towards the idling car. The wheels began to spin in the soft mud, but just as I thought my former captors were they themselves going to be trapped in the inky darkness with me, the car lurched backwards to find a purchase on the pavement. My howls of anguish chased the retreating sedan as I watched the tail lights quickly grow closer together until they became as one, then disappeared entirely.

Alone. But not truly alone, as I always had a friend, a friend named Hope. Hope had a very small, quiet voice, that would increase in volume and intensity whenever we would hear an occasional vehicle approach, only to grow quiet again when the car would not slow or stop. Quieter every day as my strength began to fail me, but never totally silent.

Hope was eventually joined by a new but unlikely friend, Procrastination. Procrastination whispered, "put off giving up just one more second". That second became a minute, minutes became hours, hours became days, until one of those days I heard a different sound approaching. It was two motorcycles, but unlike motorcycles that had passed before, these had a civilized howl instead of a dull thumping roar. Hope immediately raised her voice, only to be quieted once again as the bikes flew by and disappeared around the next curve.

Was this my fate? A slow death by starvation? To die as I had always lived, confined, marginalized, unwanted, and alone? Even then, in the darkest hours of despair, I knew this to be untrue, as I had a third friend in that crate, Faith. Faith didn't have a voice, but instead spoke to me through an intangible feeling, a feeling that there was surely something else "out there", that surely, I wasn't worthless, but had a purpose in some vague master plan.

Even though I feel that I had truly reached the end of my

rope, I had no choice but to tie a knot and hang on. Just one more day.

Dad: Life Flight

Two days after Thanksgiving, I lay dying in the vastness of the Ouachita Mountains. My son Zach and I had been camping and riding our Suzuki DR650 motorcycles across the wilderness, both weighed down with our gear like a pair of gypsy vagabonds. One particular section of trail was so enticing that I just had to go back and ride it again, while Zach wisely waited at the bottom of the hill for my return and we would continue our trip west.

Crossing this trail were what we call "water bars", small dirt berms that cross the trail whose purpose is to divert water runoff and prevent erosion and excessive rutting. These ridges of earth also serve as excellent ramps for an overly-rambunctious middle-aged man to "catch a little air". Just like an airplane, lift off is important, but a safe landing is vital, and when I touched down, my bike was wrenched to the left, I was lofted to the right.

A body in motion tends to remain in motion until acted upon by an outside force, in this case a recently-sawn hardwood stump roughly the size of a gallon paint can. It impacted me, or I it, to be more accurate, on my left lower abdomen, knocking the wind out of me. After a brief period of reflection in which I pondered the error of my ways, I rolled off of the stump to attempt to catch my breath. Nothing seemed to be overly amiss, no broken bones, the bike seemed to be just fine languishing on her side in a state of repose, so I stood her back up, got myself squared away, and continued down the hill to meet Zach.

Little did I know that I had ruptured my colon, and the remnants of Thanksgiving dinner were turning my abdominal cavity into a septic soup pot.

We rode on for hours, when suddenly the pain began to build like someone was twisting a red-hot bayonet in my gut; I eventually had to stop, as any movement at all, let alone the bouncing through the woods on a motorcycle, was excruciating beyond words. We had no cell coverage to call for help, and the GPS showed the nearest assistance be miles away in the little town of Mena, AR. We had no other option; Zach's job was to navigate through the wilderness to somehow find help, mine was to somehow stay alive. Words cannot describe the feeling of watching my son's tail light vanish into the trees and fully realizing that this could be the last time I would see him, or anyone, for that matter. At the same time, I felt a certain peace; I knew that this wasn't his first encounter with adversity, and if anyone could complete the mission, Zach could. I slid to the ground, and the world went away.

"I think he's drunk". A group of riders had found me lying alone on the ground and assumed the obvious. Even though I could barely speak through the pain, I explained the situation; one of the riders just happened to be an ER nurse who recognized the symptoms and leaped into action. She immediately stripped everyone in her party of their jackets and coveralls, piling them on me then getting under the pile herself, using her body heat to keep me from going into shock. I have no idea how long I faded in and out of consciousness when suddenly I saw a blue-gloved hand appear before my face, its owner snapping his fingers and saying, "stay with us".

Zach had found help, a forest ranger many miles away.

The ranger called in a helicopter, and the next thing I remember is waking up buck naked on the operating table, bright lights and a team of masked surgeons peering into my face, then oblivion. Then pain, as another set of strangers levered me from one bed to another, and I finally began to realize my condition. It seemed that I had hoses and tubes coming out of every hole I have, and that someone had even went to the trouble to provide me with a few extra ones. That's when I saw the biggie, the so-called elephant in the room:

The colostomy bag. I was NOT pleased.

Seven days and countless indignities later, they sent me home. As Jo Ann, henceforth known as "mom" will attest, I am NOT a good patient, and I don't have any idea how I would have made it without her. My incision needed repacking three times a day, and then there was the issue of my constant new companion, that shiny plastic bag fastened, remora-like, to my side.

This was not a good time to be a resident at the Casa del Whackos.

Depression became an issue; I mean, I felt like a semi-human Pez dispenser, but instead of delicious candy treats, I was birthing cute little turds out of a hole in my side. I dropped another ten pounds in addition to the twenty I had already lost, as you find that you're a lot more careful about having that second biscuit when you know that you'll be seeing it again, up close and personal, in the not-so-distant future.

It was during this time that I decided to take a little two-wheeled Prozac. I had two Honda motorcycles in the garage, a 1989 CB1 and a newer CB500X. Even though it was a nasty day in January, Zach and I geared up against the weather and any sane counsel and went for a little ride.

It was a ride that would change everything.

Charlie: No Easy Way Out

It's time we stop, hey, what's that sound
Everybody look what's goin' down

Hey! What IS that sound? That sounds like those two motorcycles that passed a while ago, but this time they're slowing... now they're stopping! But why? Not that it matters, as nothing could be worse torture than utter confinement and neglect; if they would just release me from my crate, I'm sure that I could somehow make it on my own.

Footsteps approaching, the black gumbo sucking at the black boots; the latches rattle and suddenly the metal door to my crate swings open. Hands reach out and I recoil, but these hands are different than those I had infrequently encountered in the past. These hands somehow know how to touch a dog; not overly delicate, but also respective of my weakened condition. There are four of these hands, belonging to two humans dressed alike in what I will learn later to be motorcycle gear. They converse for a short time in a strange language, one that I would give anything to understand, then mounted up on their motorcycles and roared off towards the south.

Before I had time to grow truly concerned, they returned with a bag of dog food. Evidently, they weren't as friendly as I had initially thought, as they were extremely miserly with their newfound bounty. The stingy knuckleheads would only let me have a few tidbits at a time when I was fully prepared to dive headfirst into the bag.

Then they did something that truly shook any remaining faith I might have had in humanity; they closed the bag, loaded it up on the larger of the two bikes, and once again sped away. True, they did leave me free of my crate as I had initially hoped, but they had also caused Hope to once again raise her voice, only to just as quickly silence it, this time possibly for good.

Hope deferred maketh the heart sick, and although I was free of my crate, I saw no alternative than to return to it; although it was evil, it was an evil I knew and understood. I had been physically freed, but, mentally and spiritually, I hadn't been shown a better path, so I took the easy route and sought once again the crate's foul but familiar confines. As it was of my own free will, this time it was for good, or bad, according to one's perspective.

Or so I thought...

Dad: The Crate

Zach and I carved a path through the rural river bottoms, the twin exhaust notes of the two motorcycles echoing back at us from the dense fog. At one point we saw four forms through the shifting mist, hunters dressed in Hi-Viz orange and carrying shotguns, evidently walking out a field in hopes of flushing out rabbits. A short time later, we saw a dog crate at a small pull off area, and as we passed, could see a black dog inside.

My initial impression was that the dog was somehow connected to the hunters, and we continued on our way. When we reached the intersection where we usually turn towards home, something told me to make a second pass back by that crate. This time we got the full picture, a full-grown dog reduced to a scabby skeleton, somehow reminiscent of an old photograph of a survivor from a Nazi death camp.

No words were ever exchanged; we immediately headed at breakneck speed for the nearest source of food, a Family Dollar store many miles away in Wrightsville, AR. We returned with a bag of Gravy Train to find the dog still by the crate, so we began feeding her a bit at a time, a pace with which she was obviously not happy.

So now what? Even under the best of conditions, I wasn't prepared to carry an adult dog on a motorcycle, and these definitely weren't the best of conditions. She was so frail that it looked like she would break in half if I tried to pick her up, and I was also still getting acquainted with my other passenger, Rollo Remora, the Colostomy Bag. We had no choice but to leave her and head home to get Zach's truck, hoping against hope that she would still be there when we returned.

Then things went pear shaped; the CB1, being an older bike without a fuel gauge, ran out of gas, prompting a delay in search of a gas can, then gas, then returning the gas can to its rightful owner, which made what should have been an hour long round trip into a three hour ordeal.

When we eventually arrived back at the crate, there was no sign of the dog. Then as I walked closer, my heart sank as I saw her lifeless form in the weeds beside the crate, and I knew that we were too late. As I stopped to consider what to do next, a heard a sound that would not have been welcome under any other circumstance: a quiet but distinct growl. I thought "if you have enough strength to growl, you have enough strength to live", and Zach and I got her up and moving.

Zach put some food in the back floorboard of his Nissan, and when the dog reached in to eat, I lifted her back legs and hoisted her into the truck, and we headed home to the Casa del Whackos. To say that the trip was "aromatic" was the understatement of the century, as the dog actually smelled like death warmed over; as mentioned, it was a frigid day, and the combination of dog funk, enclosed area, and heater set on high combined to create an unholy miasma not unlike that of the devil's armpit.

We started calling her CB, or Charlie Bravo, since we had been riding Honda CB motorcycles when we found her, and the name "stuck". By the time we reached home, she had already begun attaining celebrity status, as Zach's fiancée, Tara, was waiting on our arrival, as was mom, then it seemed like every motorcycle friend I have showed up to pay respects to this wretched wreck of a dog.

As joyful as the occasion was, I couldn't help thinking to myself that we weren't out of the woods yet; she still had a long road to recovery...

But there is always Hope.

Charlie: A New Day

What is up with this? I have seen more people today than I have seen in my entire life! Although highly unusual, I must admit this level of attention is more than a little intoxicating, but I'm so weak I can only take it in small doses. The one they call "mom" has no qualms about leaping into action and has noticed that I'm having difficulty walking due to the condition of my feet, and has decided to perform an emergency pedicure. Like most dogs, I'm not a fan of my feet being messed with, but I'm really too tired to care. The warmth of a blanket coupled with the hypnotic hiss of a propane heater lulls me into a state of semi-consciousness, and the world fades away.

I awoke in the middle of the night to realize that I was once again in an enclosed area, but this one was very unlike my crate. It was full of intoxicating smells; not just other dogs, but also the pungent odors of gasoline, WD40, chain lube, and other chemical smells. Although it was dark, there was enough moonlight streaming through the window to illuminate the outlines of the motorcycles and the shape of the human they call "Zach" in a sleeping bag on a cot beside me. Eaaasy does it; his bed looks comfier than mine, so I ease up there with him, and that is where I stayed the rest of the night, even long after my extreme state of funkilisciousness had driven him back into the house.

I think that it was that first night at the Casa del Whackos that cemented my habit of commandeering any sleeping situation I find myself involved with, a habit that continues to this very day.

"Mom!!! Leave that dog alone! At least give her some time to get acclimated!" This was dad; as usual, mom ignored him and continued upon her self-appointed mission of cleansing the funk from my person. She and Alex gave me the full spa treatment, lather, rinse, repeat, until the filth from my body was circling the drain like some sort of foul whirlpool.

After the bath, more wonder was to appear, this time in the form of a gruel consisting of puppy chow, evaporated milk, and raw eggs that mom whipped up in a blender. After a bit of this otherworldly delight, I clicked my way into the living room to find dad sprawled out on the couch watching football with Zach. If the furniture was good enough for them, it was good enough for me, so I then completed the next stage of my eventual takeover as benevolent dictator of Queen of the Casa; like the cot, the furniture was mine as well.

I eventually introduced myself to the other inmates and future compatriots in our bid for world dominance: Echo the Perpetually Guilty Doberman, two mouthy Finnish Spitz named Mia and Angel, and a dignified but slightly rumpled older gentleman named Max E. Million. They gave me a full debriefing on the tactical situation as follows: although mom was not to be trifled with, dad was a complete pushover, and Zach and Alex could be used as allies as well. Any attempt to attain hierarchy at the Casa was to be first decided by establishing territory on The Bed, which would then extend throughout the rest of the house.

This is when I began to formulate my plan for world dominance: first the bed, then the Casa, then Arkansas, my influence spreading insidiously across the globe until it would be too late for any other usurper to rise and challenge my legitimate claim to the title of Charlemagne Bravissimo!

Until then, I must be patient and contemplate this while I nibble my butt.

Dad: The Story Spreads

Due to mom's strictly enforced dietary regime, Charlie's condition began to improve. It was during this time that two extended family members, Hannah and Tania, started a Facebook page chronicling her recovery. I was unaware of the scope or reach of the page until the first day we took Charlie to the vet, when Dr Andrea asked if she could tell people that we were actually there.

Do what? Unless it was my Ichabod-like boss checking up on my whereabouts, who else could be wanting to know if we were actually present at our 1330 appointment? As it turned out, the phone lines were jammed with people from across the country inquiring as to Charlie's status, and probably checking the veracity of the story as well.

Although her condition had improved, she wasn't out of the woods yet; her extended incarceration left her with liver and kidney issues, as well as extensive damage to her skin from the constant contact with the toxic interior of the crate. Charlie only weighed eighteen pounds, and it was impossible to determine her exact age; although she had the teeth and jaws of an adult dog, her body showed no sign of ever having been through even one heat cycle. Whether this was due to lack of age or prolonged malnutrition will always be a mystery.

My "slightly touched" Uncle Larry suggested that I start posting updates on Charlie's recovery and acclimation process from the dog's point of view; little did he know that she had already shanghai'd my iPad and was doing a little writing already. She had gotten weary of seeing the constant barrage of negative stories as presented by social media, and decided to tell her own story, never concentrating on where she had been, but instead of where she was going.

Charlie began to formulate her own message:

The Message of the Crate.

She hypothesized that we all have crates; that crate might be a cubicle in a dead-end job, a marriage to an abusive spouse, a chemical addiction, a negative body image, basically any confining condition that someone else might witness and wonder why anyone would allow themselves to remain in that foul situation. One could be freed from a particular crate, but if they weren't given hope and shown that there is a better way, they would find themselves returning, if not to that particular crate, another one exactly like it.

So now she travels the country on the back of the very motorcycle from which she derived her name, commenting on her observations as we ride and spreading her message to anyone who will listen, and even those who would rather not. When she's REALLY convinced that she's right about something (which is most of the time), she has an especially piercing bark that is known as a "CHARK!". Her motto, "Chark diem", is a loose derivative of "carpe diem", Latin for "seize the day", as that's what she does.

Yesterday is a cancelled check, tomorrow is a promissory note, but today is cash in hand, and every day is a gift, which is why it's known as the present. The following chapters are about Charlie's ramblings, both physically and literary, as we go when and where the front wheel takes us.

Hey, Charlie, want to go for a ride?

CHARK!!!

Dad: The Story Spreads

Many that have followed my progress from the beginning have speculated how my past will affect my future; physically, there is little to remind anyone of my life in the crate. My coat is coming in nicely, the muscles rippling beneath my skin, the only apparent flaws being the patches of skin where hair still refuses to grow due to the constant contact with the interior walls of my former prison.

There is little resemblance between the shivering hunchbacked little hound of then and the sculpted Nubian princess of today, a testament to what a just a modicum of love and attention can do to counter a lifetime of neglect.

Emotionally and socially, I'm still a work in progress. Due to my solitary confinement, I have never learned how to communicate my needs other than with my bark, and never learned how to express my affection without using my teeth. I sometimes don't realize the overwhelming power of either, although dad's eardrums and forearms bear witness to my incessant attentions.

Understandably, I despise enclosed places, although I absolutely love going for rides in the car. The scruffy one known as "Max" is an absolute master at determining when and where dad is going for a drive and I have learned much from his ability to materialize inside the car without activating dad's radar. By the time that he realizes that he has two hairy stowaways on board, it's too late; once again, our will has prevailed. And where are we going? It matters not; what does matter is that we're moving, new adventure, new experiences, every trip, no matter how seemingly mundane, potentially erupting into a party.

Life is just like those motorcycles lurking in the garage in anticipation of spring: without forward movement, they just fall over, and there is no more disturbing sight than a motorcycle laying on its side.

Max is totally satisfied with the car, but someday, I will be on one of those bikes. After all, I AM Lady Charles of the House Whackistan, and as you will see, I always get my way.

The Gospel According to Charlie

The dad is my servant, I shall not want

I maketh him to lie down without covers, I hoggeth the bed with the others.

He restoreth my roll: he taketh me on the motorcycle when he would ride solo.

Yea, though I wreak havoc when others would slumber, I will fear no evil: for I am the Charlie; dad's bark and his bite, they amuseth me.

He preparest a table before me in the presence of mine other inmates: he anointest my head with Frontline; the toilet bowl runneth over.

He leadeth me beside dewy grasses, and waiteth until I do my business, yea, even if I am eternally indecisive as to the ordained location.

He casteth me into outer darkness, only to letteth me back in with weeping and wailing and gnashing of teeth, as I shall importunately charketh to the heavens until my will is fulfilled.

Verily I sayeth to thee, she that tooteth not her own horn getteth it not tooted.

Surely goodness and mercy shall follow me all the days of my life: and I will dwell in the Casa del Whackos for ever.

Max E. Million: The Story of Max

Max here; Charlie's moping around the Casa as dad's out of town, so I finally got my chance to Shanghai the ipad. As with Charlie, my story BC (Before Casa) is unclear; there had been some puppy mills shut down in the mountains of North Arkansas, with a rash of abandoned dogs resulting from people trying to ditch evidence.

 My sister and I were found in an abandoned house, screaming, not barking, in hunger, even now I've got a biiiig mouth for such a small dog. Dad was convinced at first that I was mentally damaged, as I lay unresponsive next to his leg for the long trip home; we stopped at an abandoned car wash so dad could assess the damage before introducing me to mom. The dog that jumped out of the car that afternoon was not the same dog that climbed in that morning, and it's been a party ever since; everyone claims I hit the dog lotto jackpot when I took up residence at the Casa del Whackos.

I've been to the Smokies, the Atlantic Ocean, the Rockies, and all over the Ozarks, I sleep where I want, eat what I want; all I ask is that dad be in the immediate vicinity, as I still have separation anxiety. I do have to admit that I was alarmed at all the hubbub when Charlie entered the picture, as I was used to getting all the attention, but things are starting to sort themselves out. I love road trips above all else but have absolutely no desire to ever saddle up on a motorcycle.

Where Charlie is boisterous and carefree, I'm much more cerebral, always thinking three and four moves ahead to ensure my wishes are fulfilled; if dogs were games, she would be checkers, I would be chess. When we're out in the woods, Charlie takes off in a thousand different directions on a million different missions: while I do like exploring, I always have my radar-like ears turned backwards so I can keep tabs on dad's location at all times.

On a recent trip to Colorado, I found a delectable new treat: marmot poop, always better when consumed above 12000'. Mom must be a huge fan as well, as she kept trying to chase me down and take it from me; I swear, woman, find your own! I must have skipped "share" day in kindergarten. The only thing more fun than snarfing it down is yarking it back up, especially in the confines of a jeep where all in proximity can share in the experience; dad, mom, Craig and Levi must have been under inspiration to find their own cache of poop, as they all immediately exited the vehicle, Levi even tossing me out of the window, evidently under the delusion that I would go find some more for him; as if!!! It is amazing how much more realistic dried marmot turds look coming back up than they did going down; try it sometime if you don't believe me.

If you're out on your travels this summer, give us a shout; we'll leave the dog bowl out for you...

Charlie: A Plan is Hatched

Dad made the mistake of letting me stay up to watch Game of Thrones tonight, and all the political posturing has caused me to begin formulating a plan of my own. The whole affair began with a few minor skirmishes, with mom trying to exert her dominance by sentencing me to political exile by banishing me to the foot of the bed.

Well, that wasn't going to work for me; I had spent too long being trapped in that crate, so long in fact that even after being released, I still would curl my feet under me when I would begin drifting off to sleep to fit inside it's invisible confines. The situation began to instigate bedroom friction between mom and dad (and not the good kind) when I would relax and begin to expand across the bed like a black lava flow engulfing all in its path.

To this day, I have no idea why mom had such an issue with the new sleeping arrangements, as dad was the true sufferer in the Battle of the Bedspace; mom would be snoring peacefully, unmolested on her barren wasteland to the east, while the only thing that was keeping dad from plummeting to the floor was his ability to clutch the edge of the bed with his butt cheeks.

Then it occurred to me; if I could so easily conquer my portion of the bed, what could possibly stand between myself and world conquest? Who needs to be the Mother of Dragons when I'm a literal Dragon myself? This is when began forming alliances with other dogs around the globe, and I also wrote my first manifesto to get things started in the right direction. So, without further ado, here's my first decree:

"By my paw, I hereby proclaim the results of the 2016 Treaty of the Bed; until the end of days, or until the bourgeois peon (dad) decides to relocate his fiefdom to the couch, Lady Stephania of the Bridge shall retain all lands north of the Tropic of Capricorn, occupying these lands with no regards as to the indigent population she has displaced. Max the Mountain Dwarf will maintain his current subterranean domain, with any and all territories under the covers subject to the whims of his iron will;
 Being of the nomadic Northern tribes, I, Charlemagne Bravissimo, bequeath unto myself the right to migrate to

and trample upon any lands I deem even remotely interesting, especially if those remote, rocky territories at the edge of the earth are being currently occupied by Dad; his carcass shall be used as the first line of defense to shield the legitimate heirs of the Land of the Bed from the dragons that lay in wait in the catacombs below. Mia the Imp shall be granted temporary visa to enter these lands and pay homage from the distant Kingdom of the Ice Queen (mom), but shall be forced back into exile posthaste when her late-night antics become unbearable (Mia's, not mom's). This treaty shall be legally binding until the cockcrow, or until I decide to change it, as this is the right I bequeath upon myself; I am aware that I've already used "bequeath" on this parchment, but I don't care, as I'm the Charlie and I happen to like the word.

Thus sayeth the Dad; no more Game of Thrones before bedtime for CB, or I will be mounting my own pre-dawn assault on castle Canine...

Dad: Stevie's Saga

Dad here; well, that's just like Charlie to get all wrapped up in hew dialogue and get ahead of herself. In case you missed it, she mentioned Lady Stephania of the Bridge in her manifesto; that would-be Stevie Mae, and this is her story.

Charlie had been the queen of the Casa for a few months, but I continued to routinely patrol the remote river bottoms where we found her crate. I was coming through the area late one afternoon when I saw a flash of white disappear into the brush near an old bridge. I stopped the bike in time to see a janky-eyed boxer mix eyeing me(I think, as one was never quite sure which eye was looking where) from the weeds. She appeared to have a dog tag hanging from her neck, but upon closer inspection, it was actually a severely engorged dog tick; in fact, even from a distance, I could see that she was infested with them.

I tried my best to coax her closer, but she was not to be convinced; Zach and I were leaving town the next day for a ten-day motorcycle camping trip to Colorado and beyond, so I had to put her out of my mind.

Fat chance of THAT happening.

When we returned, she was still frequenting the snake-infested area around the bridge but had became even more apprehensive of humans. I noticed that someone had been putting food out to entice her, and probably made the rookie mistake of trying to grab her, with negative results. As a matter of fact, many advised me to do the same, as multiple attempts to woo her closer failed repeatedly, but snatch and grab is not how we roll at the Casa del Whackos.

It was on a hot, steamy, July morning when she appeared a bit more calm than usual. The crickets and frogs that had set up housekeeping in the swamp had quite the symphony in rehearsal, and the old girl came closer than she ever had, but never close enough to give her some ear lovin's. Finally, I grew bored, sat down on the ground and started playing some tunes on my phone, notably "Change It" by Stevie Ray Vaughn. I don't know if it was the song or the fact that I was totally relaxed on the ground and on her level, but evidently that's what she needed to see. She eased up behind me and laid down, only the very tip of her tail twitching.

After a few minutes of serious negotiations and ear rubbing, she agreed to climb up in the back seat, and the name Steve Mae just seemed to stick. By the time we arrived back at the Casa, a complete transformation had occurred, and she was tearing mindlessly around the back yard in a paroxysm of sheer joy. There was no settling in period, but from the very beginning she was a perfect fit at the Casa; strong enough to contend with the force of nature that is Charlie, but more than gentle enough to not upset Max or the two red dogs.

My daughter Alex, ever the caregiver, spent the better part of that morning performing the unenviable task of hand picking the ticks from Miss Stevie, which we then baked into a delicious cobbler with a warm flaky crust. After a warm bath and dip, Stevie immediately took her place upon the bed as an official inmate of the Casa del Whackos.

Actually, I made up the part about the delicious cobbler, but the rest is absolutely true.

Stevie Mae: My Side of the Story

This is a stone-cold trip; yesterday morning I was hanging out at my bridge, now I have my own villa at the Casa, complete with hay bale and hot tub. I had adapted to life in the wild, as the bridge provided shade and shelter from the rain, but it also sheltered a lively population of fat black water moccasins, clouds of mosquitoes, and other sundry swamp creatures. An occasional human would stop by and offer a feeble attempt at victuals, usually fast food scraps of one type or another, and not unlike the male of most species, most would think that this granted them groping privileges on the first date.

Well, this girl doesn't roll that way, so they would do what most do when their advances are spurned and would tuck their tails and retreat. At least, until this mouthy little guy started showing up the mornings and would hang out for a while to discuss the issues of the day; we would have a snack of cheese together, then off he would go to do whatever it is short mouthy guys do, and I would go explore the bar ditches and abandoned houses in the area. Although very distrustful of every human's motives, I actually began to look forward to these visits, and after a few more, decided to take a chance on some physical contact. Just freaking wow; if I had known that ear scritches felt this good, I would have been indulging in this peculiar custom a long time ago.

The guy I would come to know as "dad" convinced me to climb up into the back seat of his car, and I soon found myself far away from my previous wilderness dwelling.

So now I have my own not so private place while I'm getting to know the other inmates of the Casa del Whackos. This is how I see the pecking order of the tenants on the other side of the chain link: Charlie Bravo: she appears to be the queen of the Casa, though it must be based on brute strength and hyperactivity, it sure can't be based on diplomacy, as she only has one approach and that's full-frontal assault. Then there's Echo the guilty Doberman; pretty passive until her space is invaded, then the wrath of Anubis is unleashed. Angel the matriarchal Finnish Spitz, and her daughter, Furio the mentally challenged and Mia the Spazcrobat, all Finnish Spitz and mom's favorites.

And then there's Mad Max, the only male in this particular menagerie and in a class of his own. A scruffy terrier mix and a rescue from dire circumstances, he has been dad's favorite for years, traveling with him from the Rockies to the Smokies, from the beaches to the desert. I can tell he has serious issues with the sudden shift in attention from himself to Charlie. He's the only inmate that gets to spend the day languishing inside enjoying the AC. although they all seem to come inside at night, although these tend to be pretty rackety times at the Casa. This is going to take some figuring out.

I hear it's always a party at the Casa, and it just might turn out to be true.

Charlie: We All Matter

Total peace in the predawn hours quickly descends into pandemonium as I decide that Max looks a little too smug and needs a little Bravo assault; it ends as quickly as it begins as dad enters the fray. His superior firepower, combined with a willingness to use it, make us both humbly mum, and quiet once again reigns supreme.

I can't help wondering what sets me apart from the literally hundreds of animals rescued by mom and dad over the years, or even the countless millions saved daily by rescuers like you around the world. I am the same dog I would be with or without the publicity, the same qualities and faults, habits, good and bad: it seems to me that we need to realize that we all have an inherent greatness within us.

Dad was talking earlier to a cohort in Utah who said her son wanted to be something BIG; no doubt conditioned to believe that those that occupy Oprah's couch or appear in Red Bull ads are somehow more important than those that go through life taking care of the little things until the big things come along.

When dad was designing my T shirt, "no dog left behind" seemed to fit the theme, but I lobbied heavily for "we all matter"; if the cretin who dumped me had believed these words, I would have never found myself trapped in a crate. But at the same time, without the adversity, I may have never found myself at all, just going through a short, possibly violent but definitely lonely life, never knowing what was just beyond my range of vision. I'm certainly not going to thank her for dumping me in the crate, but being mad at her is like being mad at all the evil in the world; why curse the darkness when you can light a light?

Whether canine or humane, every being seeks acknowledgement, but the only way to accomplish this is to have a mission, a job to fulfill. Even in my darkest days inside the crate, I always had a feeling that there was something else "out there", not just in the physical sense, but that I had a great calling on my life to make a difference. I didn't know how to fulfill that drive then, and, to be honest, I still am unclear on it today.

But until the Big Dream reveals itself, I have decided to follow the path of many small dreams. I will continue to use my new-found skills at manipulating dad's smartphone to continue spreading the message that there is a better way; that no matter how insignificant we consider our own contributions, we all matter, and we all make a difference.

Charlie: They're baaa-aaack...

Sunday mornings at the Casa usually find dad trying to defend his meager sugar stores against the swarming hordes of feathered micro velociraptors; while I am destroying the morning quiet with my horking, charking, and galumphing around the back yard, Stevie is most content to hang out on the deck, one eye on the feeders, one janky eye on dad. So, when the hummingbirds are in attendance, you can count on Stevie to be there as well, although she does nothing to discourage their foraging.

Some look at hummingbirds as cute little symbols of summer, but dad sees them for what they really are: at best, tiny habitual welfare recipients, at worst, well, only he knows what the antisocial little devils are truly capable of. How does something so small and active manage to poop the equivalent of their own body weight every ten seconds? Dad suspects that the hummingbird clan that frequents our feeders harbors a deep family secret, that somewhere back in time a female bird had relations with a traveling yak with the bloat, and the resulting offspring were more closely related to ducks in that regard.

A few years back, mom brought home a couple of ducklings which dad promptly named Shut Up and You Heard Me, due to their incessant peeping. Sure, they were cute at first, but then they began to eat everything that wasn't nailed down and began to grow like wild onions. They would meander around the backyard building up their ammunition stores waiting for the sound of the back door to open.

DAD'S OUTSIDE!!!

They would immediately file a flight plan that would put them directly on a collision course with the back porch, only to deposit their payloads upon arrival. With the whole backyard of the Casa to employ, why would they want to use the porch as their own personal porta potty? And if you ever get the chance to step in duck crap, decline with thanks, as it's a vastly overrated experience, simply the slickest substance known to man. If the Donald is truly serious about securing our country's borders, he would forget about building a wall and instead deploy flocks of ducks, geese and hummingbirds to the country's boundaries. The resulting slimy quagmire would slow progress by causing millions of twisted ankles and dislocated hips, and it would be entertaining as well; can you imagine the humor in seeing a plethora of refugees appearing to be breakdancing across the fruited plains? No? Consider that a blessing, as an overactive imagination is a curse.

Anyway, the expected swarms have yet to materialize, with the only activity so far being a few solitary scouts occasionally dispatched to the Casa to test the weakness of dad's defenses. He has been taking advantage of the lull in the action, using the cover of darkness to improve his position, stringing miniature concertina wire and arranging tiny anti-aircraft guns around the feeders, even digging micro trenches around the perimeter should the battle ever go to the ground.

And if the end of summer finds us with enough sugar left to let mom survive the harsh upcoming winter (as she uses at least a pound per cup of coffee), let it be said of the survivors of the Siege of the Casa:

This was their finest hour.

Charlie: Licking as an Art Form

My proclivities for excessive face licking are well documented, but I don't believe you can truly understand the extent of my ministrations until you experience it firsthand, and only dad and Zach have experienced the full onslaught.

I begin my masterpiece by pinning his shoulders with my elbows and settle in for the long haul, using this prep time to get my saliva glands primed and pumping massive quantities of warm, slimy, dog slobber. I then carefully apply the base coat, chin to (substantial)forehead and ear to ear, the secret being to never let this dry before adding additional layers. Then, like a painter losing himself in his art, I get progressively more dramatic in my tongue strokes; eye sockets get special attention, although eyebrows annoy me to the point that I try to remove them by nibbling them in a procedure I use when biting my butt. My tongue works as a brush, my floppy lips do duty as a roller to ensure more even coverage. When dad finally cries "no mas", I stop just long enough for him to get his face dried off and glasses back on, then it's on to round two!

Most people don't realize the origins of face licking; dogs are pack animals like wolves. When a mother wolf is trying transition her pups to solid food, she will go out and make a kill, bringing the food, securely stored in her stomach, back to the den. Upon returning to the litter, the pups mob poor old mom, licking frantically at her face to stimulate a regurgitate response; as the pups age, mom yarks meat that is progressively less digested until the pups are eventually eating fresh meat. Even after they're full grown, wolves continue to show submission to the alpha male and female by face licking, so when your dog licks your face she's either A: showing who's the alpha or B: trying to get you to cough up that beefy bean burrito you wolfed down on the way home so you wouldn't have to share; take your pick.

What dad doesn't realize is that I lick for a different reason; when he comes home from a long day on the road, I can tell by licking what he's seen, what he's eaten, how he's feeling, basically everything he's experienced throughout the day. This is how I relay through this page what he's thinking, although you do not want to know everything that's going on in that head of his. An example: a surgeon once got VERY offended at dad's comments while under anesthesia; when dad tried to apologize and blame it on the drugs, the doctor said: "Son, the things you said to me, most people wouldn't even think in their subconscious".

Now whenever dad has to under anesthesia, mom gets repeated requests to record what he says, and it's actually listed on his medical records for all attending personnel to be issued earplugs; it's always a (loud) party at the Casa.

Charlie: The Story of Mom

The story of mom: many have asked for the scoop on mom's role at the Casa; I've been saving it for today, 28 years of putting up with dad's shenanigans… simply put, if there was no story of mom, there would be no story of Charlie…

28 years ago, Dad was "encouraged" to go to North Carolina to separate himself from some bad influences that were destroying his life; unfortunately, at the time, he fell into the surfing lifestyle on the coast, and the hoped-for changes never materialized. During this time, he met this exotic half Okinawan/half German ex-girlfriend of the surfer dude he was staying with, with as colorful past as his own; Marine brat, black belt in kenpo, etc, who had decided to turn her own life around. Dad wasn't ready to straighten up and fly right just yet, and eventually returned to Arkansas, where he told his mom that he had met the girl he was going to marry.

After a series of life changing experiences, and not the good kind, dad never forgot the "different" girl out on the coast, so on a whim, loaded up his old Honda Prelude made the 1156 mile out there to see what might be seen. She was still there, had been through some experiences of her own, but agreed to go out with this sometimes-abrasive little guy from Arkansas. It was on their first date that dad suggested that they could go ahead and go through the long-distance process of phone calls, letters, road trips, etc, if mom thought it necessary, but since the outcome would be the same either way, they might as well go ahead and get married. Mom thought (justifiably, and accurately as well), "who does this cocky little joker think he is?" In dad's defense, he had let her get away the first time, and wasn't going to risk it again. Six months later, she traded the Onslow beach for the Ozark mountains and set up housekeeping with dad in Arkansas.

It hasn't always been easy, two headstrong people from different cultures, truly a yin/yang relationship; when she became pregnant with Zach, many expressed concern as to what type of mom she would be, as she has always had a dominant streak of rowdy tomboy in her. She proved them all wrong, both with Zach and then Alex, by refocusing that drive onto them, but don't doubt for second her iron will and sometimes off kilter thought processes. After all these years including breast cancer, a thoracotomy, and various other catastrophes, she still amazes and alarms dad with her resilience and sometimes crazy ideas, especially when it comes to animals; her rescue efforts over the years not limited to dogs, but snakes, lizards, ducks, rabbits, raccoons, turtles, even just recently, a salamander.

I honestly think she was born in the wrong century, as she would have fit right in on the early frontier, an example: dad was bow hunting some years ago and had lost the track of a deer that had escaped into a thicket. Even though mom was recovering from her mastectomy with four drain tubes still dangling, daylight found her crawling through the briers on her hands and knees, determined to find the blood trail; quite a sight, as you can imagine.

Everybody, whether physical, marital, corporate, parochial, is made up of various parts working together. Dad may be the eyes and the heart, definitely the mouth, some would say the butt as well, but mom is the brains, the hands, feet and backbone that allows the body to move and function. She sometimes feels like she operates in the background, but she perfectly demonstrates my message that we ALL matter, and ALL have a mission; if you think a particular part is unnecessary, try operating without it for a while.

Happy anniversary, mom; here's to 28 more.

Stevie Mae: Going with the Flow

Stevie here; I have found the iPad unoccupied as Charlie is doing hard time in the garage for frolicking in the ditch again, at least until dad commutes her sentence to time served or he decides to give her a shower, whichever comes first. Max and I are taking full advantage of her incarceration to pile up on dad on the couch without that canine force of nature intruding into every situation; sometimes it's good to have a little down time to reflect on from whence I came, and Max seems to understand the value of peace and quiet during such a period of reflection.

It has been three months since I relocated to the Casa, and I am on my way to full recovery and have finally put the era of the Bridge behind me. Charlie has her mission, and it's obvious that I have my own as well, but it's sometimes difficult to understand exactly what that mission might be. Even though my situation didn't involve a physical crate, my fear confined me just as effectively; now I'm a relaxed, smiling girl, comfortable in my own skin, secure in the knowledge that no matter what life holds in store, all things work together for the good. Where Charlie charges head first into any situation, good or bad, I have learned that it's sometimes much more effective to relax and "go with the flow"

But what is "The Flow"? Simply put, flow as being consciously in inner harmony with whatever you're doing.

When your task exceeds your ability, you experience anxiety; when your ability exceeds your task, you experience boredom. But when your ability exactly equals your task, you can achieve a state of "flow", a Zen - like condition where time seems to stand still and previously impossible tasks are somehow possible.

I think human relationships are the same, where the two dynamics are very seldom exactly equal, but one of the parties involved is a bit more attached than the other, which can involve anxiety. These dynamics can change as time progresses, with one of the parties becoming more dependent and "clingy", much like when a child grows up and starts their own life. I have witnessed this during my short time at the Casa, as the kids are "moving on" and the pain of parting is a bit one sided. The parent can sometimes feel a bit neglected, and vice versa; the same ebb and flow seems to occur in marriages as well.

But when both parties are equally involved, a sometimes-fleeting state of flow can be achieved; I have come to the conclusion that that is the basis between us dogs and you humans. We let humans operate on the delusion that we are dependent on them, but the opposite is usually the case, so we go through life together in a state of perpetual flow, giving and taking in in equal proportion. The only thing that can separate some of us is eventually death, which makes that final separation that much more painful. Our life spans are roughly 1/8 of yours, so I believe it vitally important to cram all of the living we can into the time allotted. As a portion of mine was involuntarily taken from me by my time alone under the bridge, I have that much more time to make up, and I couldn't have found a finer place to spend the rest of my life than the Casa Del Whackos.

Dad: RIP Stevie Mae

In the midst of life, we are in death- Notker I of Saint Gall, 912 AD

I'm the dad, and as the dad, doing the hard things sometimes comes with the territory. Last night, Stevie appeared to be doing just fine, showing no signs of distress before bedding down for the night where she always liked to sleep, crammed up against my left side with Charlie on my right. Around 2 AM, she woke me up with the sound of her labored breathing, but that eased after a bit after she got up and moved around, but I noticed that she was moving slowly when she got back in bed.

All appeared to be well this morning, and followed mom into the kitchen, then returning to the bedroom where she sprawled out on the floor. I was doing some reading around 7 AM when she got up and staggered towards the bed and gazed into my eyes like she always did when she wanted attention; I scratched her behind the ears, she licked my hand three times, then she fell over, kicked twice and it was over. I was in total shock; I've seen many dogs pass over my lifetime, but I've never seen anything like this.

It was a beautiful Sunday morning that day at the Casa, but I might as well have been digging a grave in a monsoon; it was a small consolation that when the other dogs where cavorting around the backyard, Charlie stuck right by me as I buried Stevie. It was as if she knew that a terrible loss had been suffered, which of course she was correct, as always.

In a previous life, I would never share something this personal, but the near-death experience last November changed some things; and you all have been like an extended family through the Charlie and Stevie sagas and you deserve to know the unvarnished truth. This is pretty dang rough; she was an awesome dog, living like she died, humbly but loyal until the very end.

****

Follow up: After extensive research, we have determined that Stevie died of natural causes; I could go into detail, but it somehow seems disrespectful and degrading, and she deserves so much more. I would much rather focus on her life, and remember that one goofy eye patrolling the room looking for snacks. It's hard to believe that she left such a legacy after such a short time, and even harder to believe she's gone. RIP Lady Stephania.

****

"If there are no dogs in Heaven, then when I die I want to go where they went." Will Rogers

Heaven to a dog is an earthy place, with tons of "interesting" smells, shag carpet on which to scoot, toilets from which to drink, and a dad that gives me his undivided attention; not sometime off in the sweet bye and bye, but right here in the now and now. If Dad does his best to provide me these things presently, why should God, in whatever form you envision Him to be, not want to provide for His children the very thing that would make them the happiest for all eternity? By this reasoning, I have to believe that someday Dad and I will be meeting Stevie again, and the only tears being shed will be tears of joy.

Book II

The Ten Commandments of Charlie Bravo

Thou shalt have no other dogs before me.

Thou shalt not closeth the bathroom door.

Thou shall not utter the "G" word in vain (go?)

Be not miserly with the belly rubs, yea, continue on until I hearken "enough!"

Thou shalt not feign sleep when I would rise, neither shalt thou rise when I would slumber.

Thou shalt not replace carpet with wood flooring, as scooting without friction is merely smearing.

Thou shalt not commit adultery (if I cannot, why shalt thou?)

Thou shalt not giveth me of the dry bread of the burger, nor of the pickle, but of the beef and cheese thereof.

Thou shalt not close the lid on the porcelain bowl, that I might quench my thirst without so journeying across the wasteland to the kitchen.

Be ever mindful that I saved you as you saved me, and testify accordingly...Amen.

Dad: Toxic Waist

Bad news at the Casa; at exactly 0328, we were rudely awakened when a train bearing toxic waste derailed in our neighborhood; hazmat teams were scrambled from all the neighboring states in an effort to contain this foul mess before it could get into the jet stream and possibly cause an international diplomatic incident by contaminating the ecosystems of nations around the globe.

Or it might have been that a thousand nervous skunks suffering from irritable bowel syndrome were holding their semiannual support group meeting in my bedroom and decided to waft a simultaneous air biscuit.

Or more accurately, I awoke to find myself at the south end of a northbound Charlie, and she had unleashed a silent but oh so deadly barrage directly into my face; a cloyingly sweet mixture of cotton candy, the output from a paper mill and the scent of the devil's armpit. The upside is that I will never be congested again, as the my sinuses are now as clear as if I had snorted an entire gram of Drano, the downside is that I'm sure my taste buds have been permanently affected, and I'll never be able to appreciate corn dogs, fried pickles, or Cinnabons again.

Charlie: Dad needs an Operation

It appears that dad is going to need another operation, and this one might be doozy; he has been searching the World Wide Web for surgeons that might possibly be willing to attempt this daring new procedure, but so far has been unsuccessful.

Compounding this issue is the fact that, in addition to finding a surgical team that will take on this case and also accept his insurance, he also needs to find a suitable donor; as most transplanted organs expand or contract to accommodate their particulate recipients, it is very important that this particular organ be as similar to his own in size and color as is humanly possible, as to not draw undue attention. Mom is already uncomfortable enough with the possible social and personal ramifications of this procedure as it is, and her acceptance is critical to dad's recovery. So, brace yourselves, here comes the bad news, and it ain't pretty:

Dad needs a new hand.

Obviously the two he has are not enough, as there are multiple inmates that require his immediate attention the instant we realize that his breathing has changed and arising is imminent. Max is the first, creeping up onto his chest and peering into his face; as if waking up to the presence of a penetrating glare and a hairy Sam Elliot-worthy mustache is not off-putting enough, I begin using my impressive black proboscis to ensure that the snooze button is not a viable option.

So, two hands, two dogs, so far not a problem.

Then Mia decides that she needs validation as well. Her usual method of ensuring dad's immediate and undivided attention is by standing on his chest, where any effort to dislodge her results in her meathook-like talons causing irreparable damage to sensitive tissue, until he CPO(commences petting operations).

In the Common Core math of the Casa del Whackos, 2+3=-1, and Max the Terminally Grumpy is the first to voice his displeasure at being neglected. This only serves to alert Echo that party time has started and she is missing out on the festivities, then mom just HAS to bring the puppy into the equation, and before you know it, anarchy reigns supreme.

So, where to surgically implant this extra hand? Dad has some ideas, but mom is lobbying for his right shoulder, as he already has an affinity for patting himself on the back; my vote is for his left rib cage, as he will be able to give me pats while driving, texting, sleeping, etc. Zach and Alex are both hoping for the center of dad's chest, in the hopes that it will have the ability to clamp across his mouth before he has the opportunity to say something totally inappropriate and embarrassing; this is a chronic condition with which he suffers, known to the layman as VD; verbal diarrhea.

I personally will veto the chest suggestion, as that hand would get so much action it wouldn't have time to perform it's assigned duty of spreading the loving's around between the inmates of the Casa!

Charlie: Good Friday!

Yesterday is a cancelled check, tomorrow is a promissory note, today is cash in hand

I know that all days are created equal, and Mondays should hold the same feeling of anticipation as Fridays, but actually they are living proof that life is all about the journey, not the destination.

What's the weekly destination for most? Saturday, of course, but when it finally gets here, we end up wasting it, either getting far fewer things done than we had envisioned or even far worse, …having less fun than already planned. Then Sunday comes, and before it's halfway begun we've already begun dreading the approach of Monday, and the cycle continues.

Dad has it in his will that, no matter what day he actually kicks the bucket in the hopefully distant future, his funeral be early in the day on Friday; that way anyone taking off of work to attend can make a three-day weekend out of it.

So, in honor of the sentiment if not the actual event, and as a weekly reminder to honor every day for the value it brings, I hereby proclaim every Friday as an official Charlie Bravo Day; I realize that this may seem a bit egotistical on my part, but I careth not, for I am the Charlemagne Bravissimo, and as benevolent dictator and monarch of the Casa del Whackos and soon the world, I reserve the right to change the rules as it suits my whim.

Max: A Typical Thursday at the Casa

Shortly before bedtime Wednesday night, dad spots a (full) 16 oz bottle of iced tea on the kitchen table; in this house, a drink of any type left unattended is fair game for poaching, but dad leaves it alone…

…until morning. When the tea is still sitting unmolested, dad declares open season and quickly slugs it down. He is in the process of ironing a shirt when mom walks in:

"Who drank my tea?"

"I don't know who drank YOUR tea, but I know who drank THE tea, and that was me!"

(Shocked)" You did NOT drink all that tea!"

"Yeah, I did; what's the big deal? It was sitting there all night"

"Uh, I put Miralax in that tea…"

(Uncomfortable pause)

"How much?"

(Another pause)"A LOT!"

I don't know how things are where you come from, but even in Arkansas, "a lot" is not a unit of measure, especially when describing a dosage of laxative. Besides, who puts Miralax in tea? Then leaves it unattended and more importantly, unlabeled, on the kitchen table? I smelled a setup (literally, as it turned out).

Well, dad had thirty minutes to get to work, and was confident he could make it before detonation; everything appeared to be working out, so to speak, when dad crested a hill only to see an overturned tractor trailer rig blocking the interstate. The presence of hazmat crews in full body suits complete with respirators was somehow appropriate.

We will now draw the curtain of charity across this episode, as you are once again guilty of breaking the First Law:

Never Visualize.

Charlie: Without a Vision, the inmates perish

After camping up in the Ozarks for the last two weekends, it seems almost odd to wake up at the Casa on a Saturday morning. Thing are as they should be; the inmates have all braved the Dew monster to go outside and tinkle, bringing our cold, wet, feet back into the house to trample dad's tender vegetation, then finally settling back into our rightful places on the bed.

The hum of the space heaters lulls everyone back into doze mode, as it's been an "interesting" week; the furnace has gone out, dad's mom went into the hospital with 75%

blockage, Katana, Mia's tiny offspring, has discovered the joys of log cabin building in the middle of the living room floor, and underneath it all, the ever-present presence of fear.

Fear of what, you ask? Who knows? When mom contracted breast cancer, it wasn't the initial jolt of bad news that was the most destructive, but the long, slow, steady pressure is what took the greatest toll. When you add in today's incessant news cycle of election coverage, "celebrity" gossip, natural disasters both real and forecasted, and one of the most insidious, the pressure from corporate America to perform, perform, perform with no end in sight, well, it's enough to make this girl just want to crawl back under the covers.

But that's when I remember my crate.

The greatest crate of all is fear, especially the crippling fear of the unknown; we all know my story, of how when dad pulled me from my crate, I tried to return to it, as the fear of the unknown was much greater than the disgust of my previous horrible surroundings. Why? Most say that it's because the crate was all I knew, but I have come to realize that there is so much more to the story:

I returned to the crate because I lacked a vision, both spiritually and physically.

My starvation was such that my physical development appeared to have been stunted, to the point that even the vet had a difficult time determining my age, and how long I was stuffed into that crate is still a mystery. This is not entirely a bad thing, as what girl wants her true age discussed anyway?

The sights and smells of that time in my life are long gone, with the exception of my vision, which is still somewhat affected. Since I can't see quite as clearly as some dogs, I sometimes have a tendency to shy from people or objects that pose no threat to me at all, like the story of the mule that kept shying away from the pile of hay. The farmer told him "you're afraid of the very thing that you should be full of!"

When dad and Zach rescued me, I was so conditioned to believe that that was all there was to life that I had no vision of what might lay beyond those claustrophobic plastic walls and steel bars; until I was shown a better way, I would keep returning to my former prison, or lacking that, find another just like it or even worse.

But that didn't happen; I now have a vision and a message, but more importantly, a mission. As narcissistic as I am as the Queen of the Casa, I realize now that it's not all about me, it's all about us; a body is the sum of ALL it's organs, however apparently insignificant, and a family is not a family without ALL its members. We all are family, we all matter, and, although the politicians and our media would have us believe otherwise, our contributions all make a difference.

And what about all these things of which we worry so unnecessarily? That's just life, and to experience life, you have to be living, which sure beats the alternative!

Dad: The Story of Miss Ellie

As Charlie had her crate, I had one of my own as well. I had been twenty years with the same company, and one of the perks of the job was a company car, which I had conditioned myself to believe that I could not exist without. As the working environment began to turn more toxic and the pressure, both real and imagined, began to ratchet upwards, I began to see the need for a personal vehicle, should I suddenly find myself involuntarily unemployed.

Unusual problems sometimes produce unusual solutions; I spotted an older car for sale on the side of the road, a one owner 1985 Subaru GL 4WD with only 63,000 miles on the odometer. Something drew me to her in spite of an alarming rattle deep in her engine, and I think that mom felt the pull as well, as she didn't balk when I brought the old girl home to the Casa. She reminded me of the little redheaded girl in the animated movie "Up", the girl that convinced the first the boy, then the old man, to go on so many adventures together. If you will recall, her name was Ellie, and she also had heart trouble, so I named the latest addition to the Casa del Whackos Miss Ellie, and this is how she remembers her story:

My name is Elmira, but Pops always called me "Ellie" for short. From the day I rolled off of the showroom floor, it was he and I against the world; with him meticulously caring for me; some even thought that my owner's manual resembled a baby book, with all of Pop's meticulous records of my services.

There was never anyone else, and I thought that there would never be anyone able to replace him; well. Life is what happens when your making other plans.

Pops passed a year ago this month; after 31 years together, to say that this old girl has felt a bit disconnected since then is an understatement of epic proportions. It was bad enough sitting alone under the carport, waiting in anticipation of I don't know what, but when they put me on the auction block, well, that was just a bit too much. I could just imagine some pimple faced Lothario buying me and doing God-knows-what pimp-my-ride things they do to old cars these days, and then the unthinkable happened: the mechanic drained my oil and forgot to refill it. He caught his mistake quickly, but who wants a car that may have run dry?

So, I'm not just an old girl, out of fashion and long in the tooth, but now my attractiveness has been further affected with a heart defect, an unsexy rattle deep in my chest.

That's when dad saw me; some things defy conventional wisdom and just feel "right", no matter what logic and reason may dictate, and he took a chance. I'm an old girl, and have lived a life of comparative ease, but it's time for a change; I have 4WD and I've always longed to use it, and after talking to Charlie last night, it looks like this could be my chance. She also warned me about her experience with "spa day", but I was not prepared for the washing, shampooing, tweaking, massaging, I even had my toenails painted in a beautiful shade of tan, but then came the big surprise.

After all this time, it's not all about me; I still have a purpose, and a job to fulfill.

Dad loaded me up with Charlie and Max and off we went towards the Ouachita Mountains, but my heart sank when we turned into the Subaru dealer; what's up with this? I was a little self-conscious rolling before a whole lot full of shiny new Outbacks and Foresters, but instead of shopping around, dad was showing me off. The young salespunks manning the lot couldn't be bothered to appreciate my unique characteristics, so off we went, an old car, an old(ish) man, and two goofy dogs on an unknown mission.

As we headed west out of town, it was comforting to have both dogs crammed into my front seat, even though dad had laid my back seat down to make plenty of room; I was being trusted with precious cargo. Then the asphalt turned to gravel and we began to claw our way upwards to the summit of Flatside Pinnacle.

The sun began to set behind Forked Mountain as the dogs cavorted around the overlook like complete idiots; if Charlie is truly serious about her plans for world domination, she had better hope and pray that the paparazzi never find her in one of these moods, as it's true that dogs (and people) in ecstasy look ridiculous.

There are some things about ourselves that we can fix, and other things that we have to let go and let others fix for us, and some things that simply cannot be fixed, so we deal with it and go on with life; one particular thing on me that is broken and will remain so, according to dad, is my clock. Time is too valuable and life is too short to pay an undue amount of attention to its passing.

I think I'm going to like this particular stage of my life…

Charlie: Dad Had a Dream

Between the two occurrences of dad's accident and me finding him, he had a terrifying dream in which he was wandering aimlessly through a very dark, brambly section of forest. He happened across an old, deserted mansion, the type you might see in old horror movies, the once white walls now showing a mildewed gray peeking through the kudzu.

Dad somehow found himself taking refuge inside this place, only to find in it no refuge at all, but a place of horror and neglect. It was an old forgotten insane asylum, reeking of stale urine and regret, a joyless Casa del Whackos if you will, but instead of being populated with goofy dogs, it was full of shuffling monsters and freaks.

Some were chained to walls, some strapped to beds, some so far gone mentally that they were allowed to wander the creaking linoleum halls aimlessly, but it was obvious that they all needed immediate help, but how to help them? They needed feeding, but what did they eat, and where was it kept? They needed freeing from their bonds, but then what? Wouldn't the unseen guards detect this as an act of insurrection and imprison dad as well? But how could someone possess the ability to assist someone in this environment and not attempt to make a difference, no matter the consequences?

As the feelings of panic fueled by his own inadequacies began to build, he happened across an especially pitiful specimen, leather restraints holding the man immobile to an old hospital gurney. The inmate was evidently mute, but his eyes conveyed despair and apprehension better than any words, and his body was covered with a mass of erupting boils, sores, and other corruption. Dad was standing there beside the cot, trying to determine what to do next, when a voice inside dad's head told him to put his hands on the man's arm.

Are you kidding me? Touch THAT nasty thing? What if he were to catch whatever disease was afflicting the man? But the voice was too strong to be ignored, and when dad obeyed and placed his hands on the infected arm. the man's countenance immediately changed from one of fear and loathing to one of peace and acceptance, and dad woke up. It occurred to him that more often than not, we don't have the tools or the talent to fix a bad situation, but the least we can do is not be afraid to touch someone, to love the unlovable.

When dad found me in my awful crate, the situation was much the same; how to help this obviously hopeless case? And wouldn't my diseases and vermin infect the other dogs of the Casa? But he remembered that dream, and the man on the gurney longing to just be touched and not feared, and then he saw my eyes:

They were the eyes of the man in the dream.

People remember very little of what say, they remember most of what you do, but they remember ALL OF THE WAY YOU MAKE THEM FEEL.

Make someone feel today; the life you save might just be your own.

Dad: The Road West...

Dad here; even under the best conditions, Charlie is what you would consider a "violently passive aggressive" sleeper, but when you move the battlefield from a bed at the Casa to the back seat of a car, well, it isn't pretty.

We rolled hard across Oklahoma, forsaking the interstate for the two lane at the little town of Sayre, arriving in the middle of a huge block party; Main street was blocked by a parade of classic cars, street racers, motorcycles, a long line bucking and humping from one stoplight to the next. Mexican food trucks lining the route,

Sayre had been recently hit with a trifecta of bad news, with the closing of both a federal prison and the local hospital, followed by the natural gas companies pulling their wells and crews out of the area, so employment has been an issue. In an effort to drum up some activity and civic pride, the city shuts down once a month and holds legal drag races, burnout competitions, motorcycle demonstrations, etc. Of course, we had to stop; some people like to observe from afar, but we tend to dive right in… fools rush in where angels dare to tread, and we happen to lead the league in rushing.

Many more miles and sleeping towns later, we realized that we had passed our last potential camp site, and at midnight, the next was still two hours away. The crackling classic country radio was an excellent companion, but did little to keep me awake, and Charlie was little help either; she promised to help me drive, but those became just empty words as soon as darkness fell.

Sometimes to most incredible revelations come at the most unexpected times, in this case in the middle of the grasslands; more on this later, or then again, maybe not, as some things don't need sharing.

Finally, no mas; we swore to forego the motel route, and with nowhere to camp, we found a spot off of the main road in Dumas TX and camouflaged the car beside an abandoned Red Cross truck, piled up in the back seat, and tried to get some sleep before pushing on into New Mexico.

Sleeping with Charlie is like living at the base of Mt Vesuvius when it erupted, but instead of a lava flow; a slow-moving mass of dog ectoplasm inexorably engulfing everything in her path.

It goes without saying that the sulphurous smells are similar as well.

Around 0300, I was jolted awake by my radar detector going off; not totally sure if I was dreaming that I was still driving, or I was dreaming WHILE I was still driving, I poked my head above the seat to see a police SUV parked in front of my vehicle; oh great, I'm fixing to get rousted(justifiably) as a vagrant. When he never emerged with flashlight in hand, I realized that he didn't even know we were there and was playing games his phone while halfheartedly trying to catch the occasional speeder to break up the monotony. Most would leave well enough alone and go back to sleep, but not Charlie; she started barking her idiot head off, so I had no choice but to stagger barefoot from the car and engage the officer.

He was a young Hispanic guy, very congenial and well spoken, and we actually ended up laughing about how well Charlie and I were hidden in plain sight. No hassles were given, and he went back to Candy Crush land and I went back to face the wrath of Charles.

Sunrise now finds us in Texline waiting for a one of our favorite Mexican restaurants to open so we can sample some of the finest burritos this side of Chama, and then the road continues west.

Dad: A Scare in the Night

Charlie gave me quite a scare last night…

Where to start? The Palisades at Eagles Nest? Angel Fire? The Vietnam Veterans Memorial? Capulin Volcano, her peak so wreathed in clouds that it looked like the old girl had resurrected to once again terrorize the valley below? And that was before noon…

We made a trip to Taos with the intention of camping close to the Rio Grande Gorge. There is a bridge there that holds the dubious notoriety of being a hot spot for "jumpers", ones that hope that the next life is better than this one and look for the answers in the rocks hundreds of feet below. I encountered this place on my first motorcycle trip, when I found it festooned with rosaries; I had no idea of the significance, so I took one, only to find out much later that it was in memorial of a suicide. Although I was ignorant at the time, I still felt terrible, so I had to make a second trip back to return it.

The highway department investigated the possibility of raising the guardrails, but the additional weight would have affected the structural stability of the bridge, so they had to settle for suicide hotline call boxes at each end; I can't imagine that being much of a deterrent for someone that distraught, but I'm sure it serves as conscious balm to the federal government (if they actually have a conscious, that is).

We had heard about some natural hot springs far down below that required a long hike, but this is the kind of thing we relish, so off we went; Charlie is a different dog out in the desert, bounding up and down the trail, slinging slobber, horking and whoofing, "dad! what's the hold up?".

I would see her way down below by the river, only to magically reappear in front of me, then gone again.

The hot springs are truly mind blowing; 100° water separated from the icy Rio Grande by a narrow rock shelf. There are multiple pools to choose from, which is fortunate, as some New Mexicans are a bit more liberal in their bathing attire than we are accustomed to back home. Charlie wasted no time making a complete nuisance of herself; you would think that a dog would not like hot, mineral loaded water, but if you did, you would be wrong, what an absolute goober she is.

We made the looong(did I mention long?) trip back up to the canyon rim, picked out a campsite with a suitable view of the next morning's sunrise, and drove back to Taos for a quick dinner at Orlando's (who knew that Jessica Alba waited tables?); went back to set up camp only to find an extended family had set up camp close to our spot, a father and son with their respective brides as well as two dogs. As I was setting up camp, I heard the sounds of a guitar coming from their camp; just so happened that I had brought the banjo, and a jam began to take place.

A group of free spirits partying in the springs far below were drawn to the clamor and began dancing around the fire pit while the stars wheeled in the crystal skies above; it would be impossible to script a more surreal or incredible happening.

The temperature began to seriously drop, so Charlie and I took our leave to bury up into the sleeping bag; she had been acting strangely, moving very slowly and hunched over, which had me worried, visions of Stevie dancing in my head; she actually took on a bit of her former appearance, the hunched over dog from the crate. Had she encountered a rattlesnake or some exotic desert thorn on one of her jaunts? When she wouldn't even be bothered to burrow into the bag as usual, I could feel a bit of panic building, but what to do? 0300 in the desert, many hours from daylight and any possible vet services? I did the only thing I could, cramming her into bag with me to stay warm (well, a little less cold), and wait for morning.

All good things come to those who wait, and the sun rose to find old Charlie wanting out of the tent to harass any potential wildlife, maybe arching and stretching a bit more than usual, but overall appearing a bit recovered.

She's now watching me break camp (not helping as promised, the shameless hussy).

Charlie: Do You Remember the Last Time You Were Truly Happy?

I do; when dad opened the tent today and the smell of the sage that we had packed in there in anticipation of this very moment flooded us with the bittersweet odor that simply means canyon country, the winds that blow from far away.

When I see dad pull on his boots, foregoing the "business casual" pleated Dockers that are neither business or casual, but are part of a insidious marketing plan to further emasculate the spirit of man; these boots mean we're GOING!!!, and it doesn't matter where.

The sun rising in our mirrors, and the sun later setting through a rainbow haze of bug guts on our windshield, the arcs painted there by the ineffective sweep of the wiper blades.

Water from a roadside spring so sweet and cold that it makes my front teeth throb.

When the ditch is running with muddy water, and dad can't keep me out of it, knowing full well that we have to get back in the car, and we don't have a towel.

A satisfying, tail twitching, unhurried poop in the high country, as long as dad can't find the camera; what is it with that guy and bodily functions?

And I could go on for days, as when you've seen life pass by from a prolonged time inside a crate, you tend to appreciate the not so little things. I have to laugh when I hear humans complain about the weeds in their yards; if all you have ever felt is hard plastic or concrete beneath your pads, even dandelions and chickweed feel like the finest Persian rugs in comparison.

People comment constantly about how happy I am, and even dad can't get his mind around it sometimes; my secret? Totally immersing myself in the moment, making a total jackass of myself if that's what the situation calls for. Do you think that those primping primadonnas and politicians that TMZ and Entertainment Tonight pimps as the "pretty people" are any happier than I? Not on your life; and what's more, I'll bet my last biscuit that they're no happier than you; it's just advantageous to the advertisers to keep us thinking they are.

I see your comments, and I look at your pages, and as a whole, you are a much happier, well-adjusted lot than even you probably give yourselves credit for, so look up; there is a time to kneel, but also a time to stand, as well as a time to frolic in the ditch, to flounce with wild abandon. If you want to see the epitome of strength and character under adversity, ignore the media and look in the mirror; you will find the inspiration you need looking back at you.

Some have said that they envy us our travels, to which I reply, "what hindereth thou?" Money? We have none, so we sometimes sleep on the roadside and eat beanie weenies. Time? Distance? Health? Age? All relevant concerns, but I promise you that, in the end, you will regret much, much more what you did not than what you did; just ask dad. Writhing on the ground in the Ouachitas, turning septic from crapping out your insides while you watch your son's tail lights vanish through the trees will change your perspective like little else will.

So find what makes would happy, then do it, over and over until it becomes a habit, but not for yourself; do it for someone else that can do nothing in return, for in the end, lasting happiness lies in service to others.

And in road trips; there is that as well.

Charlie: Pekudei

It's incredible what you will hear if you take time to listen; recently dad and I were coming through the Ozark mountains late at night. Up there, cell coverage is spotty at best, and radio reception has to be set on perpetual scan to pick anything up, and even then the best you can hope for in that neck of the woods is snippets of "modern" country(yark) or, even worse, "contemporary" Christian, rather soul-less facsimiles of the very real types of music from which they both originated.

In the midst of this musical wasteland, we picked up an unknown station, the rapidly fading voice of a rabbi talking about "pekudei", the Hebrew word for counting, as in each person counts and is an indispensable part of the master plan. In fact, he stated that he tells people to quote every day "the whole world was created for me in particular".

Hello?

As the Queen of the Casa, this is something I can get my mind around; although at first it sounds arrogant and egocentric, what I took it to mean is that we all matter, and all can make a difference. A person that feels like they don't matter is much more likely to lead a life without meaning or contribution; why even try to better our own lives or that of those around us if we ultimately believe that we don't matter anyway? What's the significance of my one drop of water in a gushing waterfall?

While some might view it as a bit cocky, I personally believe that, as a dog that sees herself as the most beautiful thing in God's creation while at the same time being humble enough to realize that she is still a small part of God's creation, I will be much more apt to take my actions seriously, ensuring that I live a life that positively impacts those around me.

Which is why I take this page so seriously, at least until something fun distracts me, which happens basically every .314 milliseconds. When reading the writings of the great authors, Steinbeck, Twain, Voltaire, etc, it's easy to get disheartened; why even bother? What can a dog say that hasn't already been said already, and said better, and said without having to stop to go harass a squirrel or nibble my butt?

I have to remind myself that if we all truly matter, then I matter as well, as I'm an integral part of the greater "we"; as in "we be of one blood, ye and I."

Charlie: Mom Needs Intervention

This story takes place before I entered the picture, but it gives insight into the asylum that is the Casa Del Whackos; Dad is the mouth but mom is the legs of the operation, keeping his car stocked with dog food in the eventuality of finding strays, and she's the one that leaps into action when dad brings a dog like me home. Before moving out, Zach and Kat had always been instrumental in nursing these animals back to health and dealing with the cases that sometimes don't turn out so well. We have a pretty good thing going, never a dull moment, but mom being mom, she sometimes gets a bit carried away.

A prime example: dad comes home from work only to find a greasy little mouse incarcerated in the bathtub. His efforts (the mouse, not Dad's) to escape his holding cell make him look like a miniature Tony Hawk navigating a half pipe, his oily little feet doing a Fred Flintstone on the porcelain in an effort to reach the top and freedom. While dad is usually prepared for encountering odd sights at the Casa, this was a bit beyond the norm.

Mom had caught the mouse on a glue trap but wasn't prepared carry the plan through to its logical conclusion where the mouse transfers his address from "behind the baseboards" to "in the trash can". She read on the box where you can release the mouse from the trap by using vegetable oil to break down the glue, which proved very effective, but now what to do with the mouse?

Dad made the observation that she couldn't very well commute the mouse's sentence to time served and released into the wild, as now the other mice might mistake it for a French fry, and we all know THAT scenario won't be featured in a Disney cartoon. As usual, dad overplayed the situation and got mom feeling sorry for the mouse, then went on about his business, tinkering with the bikes, etc, returning to the scene of the crime later to find the mouse with no signs of oily trauma, reclining on a bed of cotton balls, secure in his own Casa del Terrarium.

Do what?

Mom had given the mouse a bath and blow dried and styled his fuzzy little coiffure; how she did this without getting bitten is beyond me, but as it is written, so was it done.

Sadly, no photo documentation exists of this episode, but the mouse became an inmate of the Casa for some time before meeting his untimely demise due to the actions of Uki the Wonder Dog, a story for another day: it's always a party at the, well, you know the rest...

Charlie: Hail to the Chieftess

Some have wondered why I have spent so little time commenting on the presidential circus, er, primaries; this page is about sharing the GOOD news, not commenting on the bitchiness, big hair and bad pantsuits of one of the candidates.

And I'm not talking about Hillary, or Bernie either for that matter, although both of those pontificating windbags could use a major dose of humility as well.

It's slightly depressing that it would appear that these three goobers are the best our country has to offer, although I refuse to believe it; any one of the followers of this page would make a better leader of our nation. I would even throw my collar into the ring except that I've not ready to step down from my lofty perch as Queen of the Casa to assume the diminished position of the Presidency.

I do admit that it would have its perks; of course, every Friday would be decreed as Charlie Bravo Day, my Secret Service bodyguards would be required to listen to Stevie Ray Vaughan and Johnny Cash through their earpieces, and the carpet in the Oval Office would be replaced with a deep shag so that foreign dignitaries could join me in a good scoot.

All sensitive diplomatic meetings would be preceded by a ritual of my choosing, and I'm not talking about the Hindlick Maneuver, although that is one to which I'm partial, as well as being very effective in politics.

No, I'm talking about ear rubbing.

Ear rubbing as a way to open a dialogue is vastly underrated; Belly rubbing? It's ok. Back scratching? Meh. But the ears? That's what I'm talking about; I think all negotiations should be started with the participants rubbing each other's ears, most problems would be solved before the issues hit the table.

I would pay big money to see Obama and Putin give each other's lobes a good tug; money could be raised for charity and ultimately Ukraine would be left alone. Of course, Putin might be getting the short end of that deal, as Obama has him thoroughly whipped in the Dumbo department; a more worthy adversary might be Prince Charles, but then the ear ceremony might go too long due the the square footage being covered and the networks would have to cut away to some delusional talking head explaining the historical significance, social ramifications, blah, blah, blah…

on second thought, it's actually a silly idea, and lacks merit. I hereby decree that only I be considered in all future ear rubbings, and Max can have the chest massage and butt scratchings; now THAT'S a compromise I can accept.

Charlie: Why then do you live, if you do not choose to live well?

Diogenes was a philosopher of ancient Greece; one of his best-known eccentricities was to wander the countryside with a lantern, looking for the last honest man on earth. When the wealthy investors of his school sought to control his message by controlling his funds, he promptly took a lesson from the stray dogs in the area, forsaking his beautiful home that had been provided by said investors, and took up residence instead in a large barrel.

His followers became known as Cynics, taken from the Greek word "cygnos" meaning "doglike", living for the moment, always questioning society's norms and rejecting it's foibles as means of control; I can only imagine what Diogenes would have to say about today's self-centered "celebrities" and politicians. No doubt the Grecian nobility thought this title was an insult, but what greater honor can there be, to be described as "dog like"?

Sure, I do things in public that some find inappropriate, barking too loud, hunkering when and where I want with no shame of reprisal, but also have qualities that humans can only dream of; unquestioning loyalty, unending gratitude, undying devotion.

And it seems that humans take themselves way too seriously, buying the latest motorcycle, auto, home, vacation, etc, to impress their fellow man, when they would be humbled and shamed if they realized that their neighbor so wrapped up in his own drama that he's actually paying far less attention to theirs than they might think.

Dad was questioning me yesterday about the next book, second guessing his decision to open himself up to ridicule, when it came to me; what dog fears criticism from anyone other than his or her master? If we allow others to dictate our actions based on our fear of what they might think, aren't we making them our masters by default? And doesn't that make Fear the ultimate Master? Perfect love casteth out fear, "perfect" meaning in this context absolute, complete, incorruptible, without compromise or reservation?

You know, like a dog would do it.

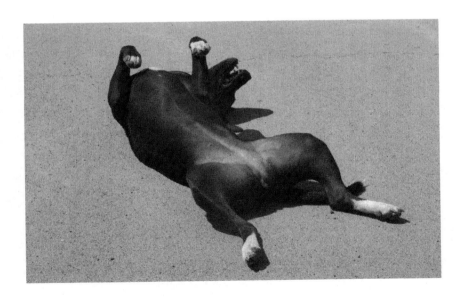

Charlie: Life's Been Good to Me So Far

Some time back, we inmates got together and scribbled this tribute to Joe Walsh on the back of a Gravy Train bag; even though Stevie has left this mortal coil, it still feels good to include the janky-eyed girl.

My name is Charlie, was trapped in a crate
A victim of cruelty, indifference and hate
two short guys on Hondas, arrived through the rain
Released me from bondage, terror and pain.

Now I'm queen of the Casa, Lady of the Bed
I hog the whole thing, and sleep like I'm dead
Dad does my bidding, that's how it should be
I rupture his eardrums when I have to pee.

I'm a new dog after all I've been through
I can't complain because I do not have to
Life's been good to me so far…

My name is Stevie, I lived in the sticks
Infested with vermin, chiggers and ticks
My left eye looks eastward, the right one looks west
The others don't matter, dad likes me the best.

I'm Mia the Nimble, the Red Spazcrobat
A younger version of Angel, not nearly as fat
I'm an ear licker, my tongue's a Q tip
I'd rather not travel, as I get car car sick.

I'm Max E. Million, the one with the beard
My mustache and eyebrows, universally feared
I'm wise beyond measure, is what they convey
The ladies all love me, that's all I can say.
Lucky we're inmates after all we've been through
The inmates not the warden are running this zoo,
Life's been good to us so farrrr…

Dad is the warden and hasn't a clue
We've got him outwitted, there's naught he can do
At home on the highway, tunes cranked on the deck
If he thinks we're not going, he needs a brain check.

Charlie: Vini, Vidi, Velcro

I came, I saw, I stuck around…

09:57; realize that dad is in The Chair; begin my ascent of Mt Dad; upon attaining the summit, claim my dominance by immobilizing his arms, begin liberally coating his face with dog spit, occasionally hooking a nostril with a canine.

10:03 hear mom rattle some plastic in the kitchen; with no regard for dad's tender vegetation, leap from the chair to investigate.

10:05 notice that dad has almost finished wiping dog spit from his face, apply a second layer; lather, rinse, repeat.

10:09 dad needs company in the shower, and I need a partial spa day after romping through the ditch, a win-win situation as far as I'm concerned

10:15 wait to get out of shower to shake, starting with popping my ears, working my way south…

10:17 …finish with my tail. After the bathroom is thoroughly moistened, go shovel-heading around the house until I realize that mom has just put a clean comforter on the bed; hooray for me! Mom is not pleased

10:22 Max looks way too smug and comfortable, a situation that calls for an appearance of Ninja Dog; Max is not pleased.

10:25 Mia the Spazcrobat proves to be a worthier adversary; hilarity ensues.

10:31 it appears things are winding down… NOT! Dad uses The Voice (I think he means it this time)

10:38 a refreshing drink from the porcelain bowl; again, The Voice.

10:45 everybody finally situated in their respectful territories on the bed, dad relegated to the barren wasteland of the far eastern territories; lights out.

10:52.5 banished to the floor; I will have my revenge, in this life or the next.

11:08 click, click, click down the hall, pause, click, click, click back down the hall, slurp, slurp, nibble, nibble, heavy sigh, long pause… slurp, slurp, slurp DANG IT, DOG, WILL YOU EVER CALM DOWN?!?

11:17 back on the bed; dad is such a pushover. Good night, John Boy…

Dad: The Inmates Take over the Asylum

This is every warden's nightmare, the moment when all control is lost at the asylum. All video surveillance systems were disabled and no alarms were sounded as all the inmates glided wraith-like through the night to their predetermined positions.

Then, pandemonium.

They say that the darkest hour is just before dawn, and this is when I was rudely awakened to find myself the helpless victim of a vicious waterboarding session at the tongues of two relentless assailants; I knew that this was no ordinary interrogation, as no questions were asked, the two taking a silent pride in their efficient but heartless task. It was obvious that they had no other motive than to break my will, my muffled cries for mercy falling on floppy but deaf ears.

Then, orders were barked from an unseen source, and the second wave of torture began; sleep deprivation, followed by another waterboarding session, then bright lights, loud noises, claustrophobia, ad infinitum; will it ever end? What do they want from me? What have I done to deserve such treatment? Were the car rides not long enough, the porcelain bowl not flushed properly?

Then, just when all hope seemed to be lost, relief arrives in the form of an Asian SWAT team(mom):

"It's past six; you had better quit laying around with those dogs already and get ready for work!"

Alas, released from one type of bondage only to be hounded into another; will the torment ever end?

At least it's Friday.

Charlie: I need to go outside and eat some grass...

...so I can come back inside and yark it upon the living room floor, as I'm sick to my stomach; just spent the last hour working on a post, only to have it inexplicably vanish, and it was a good one.

Mom and dad are tearing up the carpet in the bedroom, the stains and dirt underneath similar to the rings on trees in that they represent the passage of time; the proof of fifteen years, two kids, and countless dogs and a Casa well lived in. No regrets, but sometimes we have to let go of the past, both good and bad, so we can get on with the future.

I have been trying to be of assistance, but mom is convinced that having three dogs in attendance is somehow distracting to laying carpet, so I have sequestered myself in the living room until the carnage is complete.

Some days the words come effortlessly, but with the events of the past week, or even months, it becomes much more difficult. Then when bad events are exacerbated with shrill rhetoric and political posturing, well, it makes this girl just want to tuck her tail, take her dog bone, and crawl under the covers.

But then I remember: I have a purpose.

Remember the story of Johnny Appleseed? His real name was John Chapman, and he lived in pre-colonial America at a time when apples were in very short supply. Rather than cursing the situation as most were no doubt doing at the time, he decided to make a difference; he bought a sack of apple seeds and began sowing orchards across the northeast. He sowed with no thought of recompense, but his altruism had a unexpected result, as people began to buy his orchards, which in turn financed more orchards, and he became a wealthy man. This allowed him to engage in other philanthropic efforts, to continue to "pay it forward", so to speak.

While there is no shortage of apples in America today, this is a shortage in good news, or so those that would seek to advance their particular agendas by sowing hate and mistrust would have you believe.

Well, they may be selling, but I ain't buying.

I want to be a Johnny Appleseed of ideas; I realize that I have been given a rare opportunity and have no intention wasting it. This blog is the equivalent of an electronic bag of seeds, and it is my mission to plant those seeds with no concern for the outcome, plant the seeds and move on.

Will they all take root and produce fruit? Probably not; I'm sure some will get choked out be weeds, others will be consumed be drought while others will be washed away by flood. But if one brings comfort, or even if it doesn't, it will be worth it, as I will be fulfilling my ministry, and we all have a ministry.

What's yours?

It may be as simple as turning off the news for a day and "sacking up" with your own particular bag of seeds; don't buy into the cycle of hate and rhetoric, as he/she that angers you, controls you, I'm the Charlie, and I refuse to be controlled; I have extreme difficulty even controlling myself, so why should I grant someone else the privilege? Instead, concentrate your efforts on the good that you can do instead of the bad that is being done to others.

It sounds like the work is winding down in the bedroom and it is time to call it a night; this us my sign to crank it up a notch and drag out my most obnoxious squeaky toy and chew the ever-loving crap out of it until dad uses The Voice. By then my actions my actions will have agitated Mia and Max, and anarchy once again reigns supreme at the Casa!

Charlie: Vacilando

The predawn hours of Monday at the Casa usually have a different feel than those of a Sunday, or even a Friday, for that matter, but one thing sets this one apart:

Anticipation.

It's amazing the difference that actually setting a goal will make in a dog's psyche; in this case it's our departure next week for the west. How are we going to do it? Dad has no idea; Miss Ellie is still in the shop, and if she was released today, it would be difficult to complete a proper "shake down" period. If dad instead takes the motorcycle, that means I can't go, and THAT ain't gonna happen, as the southwest is in the grips of a heatwave. What to do, what to do?

Just go vacilando.

Vacilando is a Mexican term with no English counterpart describing the act of wandering when the experience of travel is more important than reaching the specific destination.

Make it work, and play the hand that's dealt us; if we wait for the everything to line up perfectly, or even preferably, we'll still be talking instead of doing this time next year.

When Zach was small (well, he's still small; maybe I should say when he was a sprout), he never approached other kids to play; instead, he would drag out his coolest toys and nonchalantly start playing where the other kids could see him, and inevitably they would wander over to see what was going on. This was his "low impact" approach of making friends; showing off his toys, but also inviting others to play.

That's what these trips are all about, showing off our toys, and you're all invited to play. There is no reason why anyone can't do what we do; we travel fast and light, but more importantly, inexpensively, camping where we can, usually eating one meal a day at restaurant, the rest just grazing on what we can find at roadside stands. We intend to visit as many friends and locations as possible that are mentioned in the book, but if we don't, it's all good, as we're going vacilando.

It's not about the destination, it's all about the journey, and the people, not the places, are the mortar that holds the bricks of the journey together.

My heart's about to jump out of my chest.

Charlie: Happily Content

What's the difference between happiness and contentment? One of the most evident manifestations of happiness is when dad asks if I want to do the "G" word; until we are saddled up and moving, I absolutely lose my mind. At even the slightest hint of a "go", Max and I will stand in quivering paroxysmal anticipation, never letting dad out of our sight until he opens the car door.

If you think that we consider for a microsecond the mess we carry with us at all time, the hair, slobber, dirty hooves, etc, and the effect that this will have on the interior of the vehicle, I think you are missing the picture. I have the same negative impact on dad's eardrums, with the sonic boom of my insistent "CHARK!!" rendering him deaf until the car or motorcycle starts moving.

Then it's back and forth, side to side, as if something more miraculous will immediately appear in the west while my attention is diverted by events in the east, until I eventually collapse, only to repeat the cycle again and again until dad grows irritated and uses The Voice.

This is what happiness is all about; food, freedom, frolicking, flouncing, all reasons to celebrate with wild abandon; however, happiness may come and go.

Contentment, on the other hand, is often a way of life; my realization came early into my stay at the Casa when discovered that I could relax in the knowledge that my wandering days were over. Although my happiness can be frenetic and based on the moment, my contentment is usually peaceful and based on trust.

Don't get me wrong; I still have those moments of anxiety, when I hear the motorcycle leave without me, or when dad won't open the bathroom door, or when, heaven forbid, Max gets first shot at the cereal bowl, but overall, I'm a different girl than the scrawny, scabby skeleton that emerged from the crate.

What made the difference? Love, patience, nutrition, all these things make a difference, but one of the most important?

Time.

Time heals all wounds, but time is the one commodity that you have to give itself for it to be effective.

 No matter how unpleasant a situation may be, keep soldiering on and one day it will come as a total surprise when you can look back and whatever the condition, it will be like it happened to someone else.

Just like my crate; just because it made me who I was then doesn't mean that it defines who I am now…. Thus sayeth the Charles.

Dad: Here We Go Again

Dad here; 0445 at the Casa del Whackos, and Charlie, as usual, has decided to get her lick on, but this one was different. Instead of her full bore facial assault, this one was a casual "sleepily swab the back of dad's head" lick, just enough to wake me up, which of course was her sign to go back to sleep.

I saw that Charlie's phone had new activity, so I snuck a peek and was amazed to find multiple messages in French. It reminded me of the beginning of her story when it first went viral; I had ruptured my colon in a relatively minor motorcycle incident shortly before we found Charlie's crate, and as a result had been wearing a colostomy bag.

Those that have followed this page since the beginning have no doubt tried to forget the infamous poop stories of this particular era, horrible experiences, sure, but hilarious to recount today.

In March 2015, Charlie's recovery was progressing nicely, and her story was burbling right along as I was feverishly awaiting the scheduled colostomy takedown operation and a blessed return to "normal", if anything is ever normal when you pass fifty.

I was utterly dismayed when a freak snowstorm postponed the procedure for a few days, which might has well have been an eternity as far as I was concerned; you can ask mom, I'm NOT a very patient patient. It was during this four-day interval that we witnessed the phenomena of divine intervention, or at least a good nudge from the Almighty, as Charlie's story began to spread exponentially across the world. We would see a mass of messages from South America, then the focus would shift to somewhere in Europe, then Asia, then back to the states, then on to Australia, as if something was spreading the story around the world for us.

I'm a dog guy, but a guy nonetheless; I had no intention of ever teaching a goofy dog how to post on Facebook. I was just disgusted with the stories of abuse that social media loves to depress us with only to leave us hanging, and was determined that Charlie's story would be different, focusing on her recovery instead of her injury and creating a slightly snarky refuge on the Web from the incessant crap being forced down our collective throats by those who would control us by fear and loathing.

How's that for a run-on sentence?

Well, you all know how THAT has been working out; just when the flame seems to be dying down a bit, somebody stirs the embers and it flares up again, as evidenced this morning by the plethora of posts from our friends the French. A more apt analogy might be that of a roller-coaster, click clack straining to make the next climb, only to hang for an eternity motionless at the apex...

...only to once again plunge faster than you would have previously thought imaginable.

So here we go again, but where are we going? Doesn't really matter, just ask Charlie. What does matter to her is that we are GOING, the destination vague but the progress defined. Her message of inclusion, that we all matter and we all make a difference, applies to this page as well as to each of us; we all have a purpose, and all we can do is keep moving towards it, whatever "it" is.

See you on the road!

Dad: All My Rowdy Friends

A follower of the page asked for an update on those that have passed through the Casa and onto bigger and better things; there have been so many BC (before Charlie) that I couldn't begin to recount them all, so I will limit the updates to the inmates that are AD (after devastation).

Stevie: of course, everyone remembers Stevie; I discovered her in the heat of July last year, and it took me three weeks to finally gain the trust of the janky eyed girl. She was with us for only a short time before suddenly succumbing to what we can only surmise was a case of the bloat that escalated so quickly that her death and manner of passing caught us totally off guard. I've had scores of dogs over the years, but Stevie is still in class by herself; RIP, you goofy girl.

Dash Riprock: Dash was left tied to my trash can in a pouring rainstorm when he couldn't have been six weeks old; with mom's nurturing, the little goober recovered quickly to become the de facto ruler of the Casa. He was way too special to attempt to place with just anyone, and when we found what we thought was a perfect match in Arizona, Zach and I didn't hesitate to make the trip; as we were leaving Little Rock, the adopter crawfished on us. We made the trip anyway on the gut feeling that something would present itself, and present itself it did, when Michael Steele saw the story and didn't hesitate, driving from California to Raton, NM in a time that I will not recount here, at least until the statute of limitations expires. Dash is now living it large in Orange County as Takoda Steele; give him a follow on his own Facebook page.

The there was Beau; I found Beau in the same desolate area as Charlie and Stevie, tangled up in a choke chain. After a short rehab period in which he managed to scale Mia's fence with intent to commit carnal relations, we found him a home out west of town, where he roams free today.

The result of that sordid romance was one pup which we named Katana, after Kat, who discovered that Mia was going into labor; we had no idea that she was even expecting. Katana is now ruling the roost at a friend's Casa under the pseudonym "Foxy". Since coming out of Charlie's formidable shadow, she has developed an awesome personality, perhaps a little too awesome, as she is an absolute live wire.

Brenda was the Rottweiller that was found in a ditch after being struck by a vehicle; I got her to the Pulaski County Humane Society, where it was discovered that she had her pelvis shattered. Surgery was performed, and the last I heard she was walking with assistance; I asked to repeatedly to see her through this process, was denied, then asked for updates or pictures to post on Charlie's page, nothing forthcoming either. As a result of this callousness and some other circumstances, I have focused any fundraising and awareness efforts elsewhere, and look forward to expanding this in the future.

Then after a short respite from the action, four dogs were found is rapid succession, all within just a few miles of Charlie's spot. Two of them were so similar to Charlie in appearance that I'm sure that they were siblings from a later litter, and the other two were dumped on the side of a remote road with only a half a bag of cheap dog food left as what I can only assume was conscious balm. Your donations were sufficient enough to take care of all four dogs spay, neuter, and adoption fees and it is my understanding that all four have been adopted out and transported to homes up north.

Now what? We heard yesterday that almost 50 emaciated dogs were rescued from one house in a county just to the south of the Casa. As we're leaving for Colorado early tomorrow, I'll not be able to get fully involved until we return, but I plan on calling from the road tomorrow to offer Charlie's help.

The purpose of this page is primarily to spread good news, but sometimes it becomes necessary to stop talking and start doing. The need is so urgent that it often overwhelms those of us that have the best of intentions; we can't fix every problem, but we can work to alleviate the situations that are placed in our paths.

Tomorrow we ride to the west; stay tuned!

Charlie: Dateline South Mineral Fork, Colorado

We been on the road since Friday. Usually it takes a few days into a journey to find your "mojo", or the particular rhythm of the road, but this one seems to be a bit more difficult than most. Small hindrances have kept cropping up, nothing major; intermittent rain and hail, a touch of altitude distress, and then there's the crowds. You would think that it would be difficult to get claustrophobic in an area as vast as the Rockies, but the 4th of July seems to bring out the hordes in droves.

The first part of a journey usually tends to be about the places, with the latter part usually being about the people; this trek seems to be exactly the opposite, with encounters too numerous to mention in this post. In addition to the planned encounters with the sisters of Our Lady of the Desert and the outstanding family at Fina's, we shared campsites with a couple of through-hikers, Mark and Monique, as well as a family with a beautiful autistic son and his gentle but protective Rottweiler. Each meeting was worthy of its own post, a situation that we will remedy at a later date.

It's the little foxes that spoil the vine, and even the most spectacular of surroundings can be obscured by expectations that sometimes are a bit too lofty. Tired, grumpy, smelly, almost like an unholy trinity of Snow White's dwarves, we decided to turn in before the sun had even set behind the mountains.

A king size bed is roughly 7' across, and I relegate approximately 18" of this to dad when we're at home at the Casa. A Thermorest sleeping pad is 20" in width, and I see no reason why I shouldn't keep the ratio constant; I'm sure that the Big Agnes sleeping bag company would probably void any warranty if they knew to what extent I tested their seams with my battle for sleeping supremacy, but we finally reached a compromise, nested together like a set of Russian eggs.

The combined output of two sets of snoring lungs raised the humidity level of the tent to that of a tropical rainforest, and the steady drip of condensation on dad's head served to rousted him from his slumbers; I had no problems in this area, as I was burrowed own behind his knees.

The "zzzzzzzzz" sound of dad opening the tent fly caused me to extricate myself from my cocoon of nylon to find an absolutely glorious, although frosty, sunrise. The sound of the creek burbling beside the tent had been more than sufficient to mask the sounds of another pair of campers setting up shop in the night, but they had not yet arisen, so we technically had the valley to ourselves. If you've never experienced a Colorado high country sunrise, it's indescribable, but I'll try.

The sun rising in the east barely illuminates the tips of the western-most peaks, the aspens and spruces silhouetted against the skies of both ends of the valley like alpine bookends; as the sun continues her ascent, her warmth washes down the slopes, incrementally transforming the cold grays of the valley into a cauldron of color. The remaining pockets of snow in the high cornices restart their melting process, adding the sound of waterfalls above to the increasing volume of the creek below. One almost hates to intrude on this magical scene, but the allure of caffeine beckons, so dad has to drag out the Whisperlite stove, and the day "officially" begins.

At least for him; I'm crawling back into the sleeping bag.

Charlie: Clear Lake, Way Up Yonder

We had every intention of camping at Clear Lake last night, but thought better of it when dad did the math; you lose approximately 10° for every 1000′ of elevation change, and it was in the low 40's at 9000 where we are, and Clear Lake is 12,200' with 40 MPH winds at the summit. I could just imagine our tent sailing off of the top of the mountain like a yellow hang glider with a hapless dog and old fat guy snoring blissfully inside; no thank you, I'll hog the sleeping bag down here, and we'll make the ascent in the morning.

Timberline starts at around 11,000, where all trees and larger vegetation gives way to alpine wildflowers and grasses; everything is smaller and hardier up there, but also more beautiful, the colors being much more vibrant.

With the exception of the marmots; for something that appears as pudgy and soft as they do, those little varmints have no problem darting up and down sheer cliffs that this girl wouldn't even consider, so I wisely didn't even try. Sometimes discretion is the better part of valor…

I haven't even begun to describe the wonders of Clear Lake; I dedicated a whole chapter in the upcoming book to this place, and still didn't even scratch the surface. Imagine a crystal lake hanging on the side of a mountain with even higher peaks soaring out of its icy depths, and the wind separating miniature icebergs from the shore and setting them adrift. The contrast between the azure blue of the skies and the snow-white clouds provides the backdrop for this epic panorama; photos don't begin to do it justice, but they will have to suffice, as this is a incredibly difficult place to attain. Then again, most of the best places are.

There were some heavy-duty land rovers camped just below the summit, no tents for them, that said that the winds the night before were so extreme that it almost toppled their rigs. They had a goofy rescue dog like myself, and the majesty of the place was immediately sullied by the tomfoolery of two hyperactive buffoons whose brain functions were obviously affected by the lack of oxygen. Again, pictures at a later date will have to suffice, as there aren't enough words in the English language to describe this scene. That, and the pictures are on dad's other camera, and any kind of cell coverage is nonexistent in these parts.

There is so much more to show and tell about this day; not even 1100 AM, and we still have to cross Ophir Pass at 11,789′, then on to Telluride and Last Dollar Pass before ending up back in Ouray. This week is coming to an end waaaay too quickly as the reality of life back home beckons; the bad part of living the dream is the knowledge that the alarm is always about to go off.

I believe that I'll be hitting the snooze button a few more times before this trip is over…

Charlie: These ARE the Good Old Days!

Ten years ago, mom was diagnosed with cancer, with all the associated indignities; hysterectomy, mastectomy, chemo, etc, and handled it like an absolute trooper. All is now well, and life goes on.

Eight years ago, dad ruptured his Achilles tendon playing basketball, then two years ago ruptured his colon landing stomach -first on a stump when he took a header over the bars of his motorcycle; he always emphasizes the stomach part, as everyone assumes that the stump impacted a more private area when they hear the word "colon". It was during this time that I came into the picture and we all know the sorry state I was in when I was freed from the crate.

Now here I am, tapping out these words in one of the most beautiful areas on this planet, Gothic, Colorado. Yet when I look back on pictures taken during those life-altering, difficult times, I don't see the stress or pain that was obviously involved, only the happiness; who would have thought that those times instead of these would now be viewed as "the good old days"?

As incredible as this trip has been, Gothic, Ouray, Ophir, Chama, Gateway, etc, it's hard to imagine that the memories made can even compare to those that are made on a daily basis back home, especially during what seems at the time to be "the worst of times. And as the car and our thoughts turn towards home and the mundane problems we all have to face, I am reminded of those that follow this page that are going through MUCH more strenuous tests like cancer and death while we're out here gallivanting around in the backcountry.

I often fear that this page might be taken as a bit of electronic narcissism, but that couldn't be farther from the truth; we would love to be able to take everyone along on our treks, but we all know that that's not going to happen, as dad has an odd way of traveling on the cheap that most would find insane. So instead, we aspire to do the next best alternative, which is to kidnap and drag y'all along for the ride.

And every day at the Casa del Whackos, whether on the road or at home, has the potential to be an adventure, as all adventures have the same origin:

They all start between your ears.

Charlie: Onward Through the Dog

Sunday morning at the Casa; we're back in the saddle, but don't want to get back in the rut. Dad's grandfather was a wise man who's favorite saying was "a rut is simply a grave with both ends knocked out"; even after the incredible things that we experienced last week out west, it is so easy to fall back into the cycle of work, worry, rinse and repeat.

But, you might say, "Charlie, you don't work!", which would be true as I'm the Queen, but I carry a heavier load. I'm an empathetic dog, which is both a burden and a gift; a burden as I'm sometimes acutely aware of other's anxieties although unable to affect the outcome, but also a gift, as I now know my real calling. I now have a ministry of sorts, not the type where I pontificate from a pulpit and then the first in line for potluck afterwards, but a different sort; a dog with a blog, a message that we all matter and we all make a difference.

When dad and Zach found me, it was during a news cycle that seemed to be featuring an inordinate amount of abuse stories, the kind where they love to draw you into the story and get us emotionally involved to gain "traffic" for their particular advertisers.

I do believe that we should be aware of what evil that men are capable of, but the fallacy of these stories is that they ultimately leave us depressed and unfulfilled, as they offer no solutions or resolution; I resolved to use the story of the crate to make a difference and focus instead on the good life I now lead.

Although the details of my negative origins are necessary to provide contrast, I refuse to let them define who I am today. Like me, you may be an abuse survivor, a recovering addict, or have depressive personality. We may be white or black, terrier or hound, purebred or mutt, white collar or blue, in the end, none of this matters;

What matters is how I proceed from this day forward.

What I do, or have done, or even have had done to me, doesn't define who I am; from the crate to the Casa, from the guttermost to the uttermost, I've been transformed from the emaciated mutt I was to the spoiled bed hog, the queen of the covers if you will, I am today.

But I can't stop here, or my present situation will become a rut, or even worse, simply a new crate. I have to keep moving forward, exploring new territory, as if I'm not always green and growing, I'll slowly ripen and rot.

Thus sayeth the Charles.

Charlie: Mountain Sage

One of the most incredible smells on this planet is that of wild mountain sage, and there is no better place to experience it than at the North Rim of the Black Canyon in Colorado. The canyon as it is at some points deeper than it is wide, hence the term "Black", as daylight never reaches some points of the Gunnison river a thousand feet below. The variegated rock formations lining its vertical walls are oddly reminiscent of "the leap of faith" scene in "Indiana Jones and the Last Crusade", but it's what grows at the top that I'm talking about.

Mountain sage is a non-descript scrubby bush that covers much of the landscape out west; on a calm day, there's not much of a reason to pay much attention to it, much like dandelions or privet hedge here in Arkansas. But when the wind begins to blow, the scent begins to carry, a clean, almost astringent odor that just defines wide open spaces.

But if you really want to get the full effect, you have to bruise the plant by rubbing it in your hands; dad even goes as far as to rub it on his face before donning his motorcycle helmet so the scent is intensified as he rides. He even goes as far as to pack his tent with sage before returning home so when he sets up camp, the smell of the mountains permeates the tent no matter the location, but the point is that it involves stress to bring out the best.

Dad has a friend that has recently came through a rocky period in her life; a tough divorce followed by a seemingly endless series of deadbeat dating disasters, each one more dysfunctional than the last, but now she's met Mr Right. The incessant pummeling over the last few years somehow prepared her for this next stage of her life; now she's now looking forward to a brighter future, not damaged by past experience but a better person because of it.

I have to think my previous life affected me in the same way, as I wouldn't be the dog I am today if I hadn't had to face the adversity of the crate; the loneliness, the claustrophobia, the stench, my only view off the world constricted by plastic holes to my right and left and a steel grate in front of me. I perhaps could be forgiven if the experience had made me bitter and distrustful, but that is not the case; on the contrary, I am now more thankful and determined to make the best of each day allotted to me.

Like the sage, my previous owner probably looked at me like just another weed to be ignored or worse, eradicated, never realizing the treasure that lay before her, but the tribulation of that time awoke my true personality. Now I live harder, pee more freely, flounce with more wild abandon, thrash around like a wild woman, love more openly, poop where and when I want to, and when the time comes, sleep with more gusto, unencumbered by doubt and fear. I have seen the alternative up close and personal, and I much prefer to live this way, from a lowly weed to a fragrant flower…

It's great to be queen!

The Charles Riseth in the Morning

Psst! Hey dad! are you awake?

Good Lord, Charlie, it's 0430! Go back to sleep! Mom will slap us both naked and hide our clothes if you get Mia and Max riled up!

I can't go to sleep without a bedtime story; tell that one about how you found the me in the crate but leave out all the gooshy parts.

Charlie, that's not how bedtime stories work; you know perfectly well that they are to be told at night, not in the wee hours of the morning.

Well, dad, now that you brought up the fact that it is the morning, you know it IS now officially Charlie Bravo Day, and as such, I make the rules!

That's all well and good, but how does that make a Friday any different than any other day? You always think that you make the rules!

You make an excellent point dad; now, you may proceed…

(Sigh) ok, here goes; there once was a guy who had a semi-normal life. Then he found an early Christmas present in the guise of goofy dog left gift wrapped on the side of the road, and she now rules the Casa del Whackos with an iron paw. She is a master of the guilt trip, causing him to forego many activities in which he would partake, as well as give up much food that he would enjoy, that she might have her way. His is now a remora-like existence, surviving on the scraps that she deigns to bless him with as she cruises the dark depths in search of the meaning of life, and if not that, the softest place in the Casa in which to sleep. At this rate, he will eventually cease to exist altogether and they will be forever as one as he is gradually assimilated into her vast black bulk.

(Long pause)

Hey, dad.

What now, Charles?

I love a happy ending.

Charlie: Damaged Goods

Rainy day in August; always a good thing at the Casa, as it not only breaks the cycle of viciously humid days, it also forces dad to slow down a bit. I like to GO! GO! GO! as much as any dog, but sometimes it's good to hang around the house for a bit, the siren call of the road somewhat muted by the rain drumming on the back porch. The hummingbirds are undeterred by a little precipitation and continue their violently predatory ways, but the rain seems to have subdued the yellow jackets and wasps; we have declared an armistice and will resume hostilities tomorrow.

We at the Casa have a "thing" for the underdog: the abandoned dog, the misfit person, the old car, the untrendy motorcycle (dad's excuse), but sometimes we even take it to ridiculous extremes, if you can imagine anyone at the Casa EVER doing anything over the top.

When we hit the grocery store, we usually find ourselves at the "damaged goods" bin; not necessarily as a cost saving measure, but as some sort of reminder that we all are damaged but still good. Although the can may be dented and the label torn, the peaches inside are still as good as the day they were born.

Like me, many readers of this page could be considered by some to be damaged goods; the farther the package travels and the more it is handled, the more apt there is to be superficial damage, but the key word here is not "damaged" but "good". The package does not define the contents, it merely serves as the medium of transport.

You've all seen the pictures of my rescue; the cold drizzle, the motorcycles, etc. What you don't see (thankfully) is dad's colostomy bag, the result of a freak motorcycle accident barely two months before. As you can imagine, at the time this was a MAJOR issue, one that he was sure would never pass (get it? "pass"? I kill myself), but now that's all behind him (there I "go" again). A second surgery was successful and what was once a life changing situation has left him with just a little additional damage to his packaging.

Mom's package is no different; cancer surgery, chemo, a thoracotomy, and all the associated indignities over the years have left her with her own particular physical personality. But, like yours, this does not define the contents, and to be honest, hasn't really changed the packaging that much either.

Time heals all wounds.

When I emerged from the crate, I'm sure I looked and smelled like damaged goods, not a spot on me that dad and Zach could pet due to the protruding bones and oozing sores, but that was then, and this is now. Now the only physical reminder I carry of this particular time is literally on my back; three white hairs that mark the last lesion to heal, the spot on the arch of my spine that was rubbed through by constant contact with the crate. Maybe someday these hairs will vanish as well, then again, it matters not; what does matter is that my packaging does not define who I am any more than yours defines you.

Speaking of packaging, I'm fixing to do a little damage to Mia's if she doesn't get that squeaky ball out of my face when I'm trying to finish a post; mom gifted me a new phone last night, a waterproof, shockproof Samsung Active 7, and we need some quiet time together.

Doubtful that this will ever happen until we take this show on the road, as there is precious little quiet time at the Casa.

Dad: Consider the Puppies

When Hurricane Katrina slammed into New Orleans back in the summer of 2005, the flood of refugees and their stories of despair into the surrounding states was devastating. Getting the family heavily involved in the relief efforts alleviated the stress and anxiety somewhat; doing something is always better than doing nothing.

It was during this time that I was playing basketball with some kids, lunged for a rebound and heard a BANG behind me and I hit the ground like I had been poleaxed. My immediate impression was that I had been shot in the back of the leg, but actually I had suffered a catastrophic rupture of my Achilles tendon, my foot flopping on my ankle like a beached mackerel.

The fun really began when I came out of the hospital in a full-length leg cast, and I quickly discovered that hydrocodone and claustrophobia don't make good bedfellows; I remember thinking frantically "if I could just see my toes…". After mom went to bed, I crutched my way out to the shop for a pair of tin snips and a hacksaw to perform a little cast modification which turned into a LOT of cast modification; at this point I realized through my drug induced fog that I might not have made the best of decisions and fled the scene of the crime. The next morning mom awoke to the sight of a living room awash in plaster, cotton, and hand tools, and had to take me back to the hospital to be recast; I'm amazed to this day that they didn't send me home with a cone on my head like a dog be restrained from chewing on her stitches.

This set the tone for a time of depression that lasted for months; "Wake Me Up when September Ends" by Green Day was popular at the time and became my personal theme song. I was confined to the house, Arkansas was in the midst of a drought, the effects of Katrina still being felt and a second hurricane, Rita, was already forming off of the coast. The incessant barrage of bad news on the media and my total inability to do a blasted thing about it had me pinned to the ceiling, figuratively speaking of course, as I was incarcerated in my recliner directly in front of a 27" flat screen sewer pipe spewing toxic waste directly into the living room of the Casa del Whackos.

I HATE not being able to make a difference, and you can only imagine the effect that my mental state had on mom and the kids. I'm still surprised that they didn't just wheel me out to the curb for Monday's trash pickup, but they probably knew the landfill would just send me back; it was not a good time to be a resident of the Casa.

I remember a particularly stressful day in front of the TV, feeling the surging anxiety when I noticed my dogs in a semicircle in front of me. I was eating a ham sandwich to which they obviously all felt entitled, and had their backs to the TV, oblivious to the bad news I was actually feeding on. It occurred to me that no matter what was happening on the outside, they trusted implicitly that they would be taken care of, and how much more should I trust in a Father that, unlike me, had proven time and again to be unfailing?

Now here we are again: Ebola becomes Zika, Ferguson becomes Minneapolis, Bruce becomes Caitlin, Bush/Gore becomes Laurel/Hardy, and the "crises" keep goose stepping into our lives, each making us feel a little more ineffective and disconnected than the last. But there is an answer: be not weary in well-doing, as though our individual actions may seem insignificant, together we can and do make a huge difference.

We all have something to give, but until we actually give it, it's not a gift…

…and I can't wait to unwrap mine!

Dad: Thank You

…for a good night's rest, one not marred with jarring thoughts of doom and despair or buzzing, nerve-jangling phone calls in the wee hours of the morning. Thank you for self-entitled dogs that obviously have no concept of fractions and right angles but somehow realize that diagonal and even horizontal are the ways to occupy the most real estate. Thank you for sleeping arrangements obviously engineered to help me overcome any claustrophobia concerns, the equivalent of slumbering in an MRI machine constructed of snoring, farting, dogflesh.

Thank you for providing me with an organic alarm clock who's saliva output is sufficient to ensure that searching for the snooze button is out of the question. Thank you for a wife who is understanding enough to realize that resistance is futile and it's best to just adapt and improvise, and that sleeping with her head at the foot of the bed might be considered by some as a form of canine Feng shui.

But most of all, thank you for a bunch of fellow misfits who understand my blessings completely, a family that stretches around the globe, brought together by the stories of a once sad but now sassy diva dog.

And then they all said…

Amen.

Hotel Del Whackos

On a dark southern highway
Humid wind in my fur
Out cruising with Miss Ellie
Her normal rumble a purr
I hear a bark in the distance
As dad pulls up the drive
What sounds like a cacophony
Is Mia losing her mind inside
Dadadadadada, da...
(Guitar build up)

Welcome to the Casa del Whackos
Such a lovely place, if you can find a space
Living it up at the Casa del Whackos
Where a chair is rare
not covered with dog hair.
The dogs here are the inmates
The warden? Well, that's dad
But if he thinks that he runs this place
His self delusion is bad
We dictate sleeping arrangements
Leave him with nothing but crumbs
It's obvious the inmates here
Run the whole asylum.
Dadadadadada...

This place is the Casa del Whackos
We make the rules, we cavort around like fools
Living it up at the Casa del Whackos
Our actions aren't always apropos
As our combined IQ's are low...

Water in the toilet means water on the floor
I drink when and where I want to
And sniff around for more
Max is a grumpy old terrier
Mia's my partner in crime
Angel and Echo stay out of our way
It's always party time!
Dadadadadada...

Welcome to the Casa del Whackos
The dog bowl stays in place
for the next hopeless case.
Come and sit a spell at the Casa del Whackos
You won't need an alibi
We be of one blood, ye and I!

(Guitar break, ad infinitum)

Dad: Chark Diem!!!

Dad here; I have stated in the past that it was my wish that everyone could find their own personal Charlie, but I am now seeing the error of my ways. If life is like box of chocolates, life with Charlie is like a box of chocolates infused with raw tequila, habanero pepper and more than a pinch of gunpowder. The day starts when I try to get her to go outside, and she greets me with a look of such sweetly sublime imbecility, "why disturbest thou thine superior?", then transforms into a sleek hair covered wrecking ball for the remainder of the day. One example:

Zach's motorcycle was recently stolen from his apartment, so he now stashes the replacement in the greasy garage of the Casa, a tight but workable precaution. As we have an Eastern Seals ride coming up this weekend, I went out there last night to inspect the bikes, check the tires, batteries, etc.

Now, Charlie has developed an obsession with anything noisy and motorized; if I start the mower? There she is, bounding up onto the deck with absolutely no regard for my bare feet. The Subaru? Same reaction. But her true passion is reserved for motorcycles and even the sound of the key going into the ignition is enough to transform her into a maelstrom of mayhem, and the actual sound of the bike causes her already meager IQ to half and her adrenaline to double. Her voice transforms from a "normal" bark (if there is such a thing) to a CHARK!!, an unholy, ear splitting combination of plea and demand that cannot be ignored.

So here I am, alone at the Casa with no human reinforcements, and when I crank up Zach's bike, I feel a whoomp!, 50# of black dog vaulting onto the saddle expecting to go for a ride. Although this might have been amusing at another time, Newton's law dictates that an object in motion reads to remain in motion until acted upon by an outside source, in this case the outside source being MY motorcycle. Her exuberant momentum caused Zach's bike to crash into mine, which then teetered over into the lawn mower, leaving me with a tangled mass of handlebars and brake cables and a floor awash with gasoline spilled from the carburetors. And where was the orchestrator of this disaster? Out cavorting with the other inmates, as it obviously didn't appear that a ride was immediately forthcoming.

So, I struggle to separate and recoup the bikes, somewhat successful until I try to lift Zach's bike from its position of repose; halfway through the process, the gas on the floor causes my feet to fly out from under me and the motorcycle found itself back on the floor. Thankfully, there was no further damage to the bike, as my legs cushioned its impact; pinned in a pool of gas by a 400# Suzuki for even a moment is a moment too long.

All's well that ends well and everything is now squared away and put back into what appears to be order at the Casa; the next time you wish that you had your own personal Charlie?

Be careful what you wish for.

Kid Charlie

I'm not a fan of rap, but I am a fan of strut, and nobody struts their stuff like Kid Rock. As it says in 1 Charlie 1:1, "she that tooteth not her own horn getteth it not tooted"; the next verse reads "blessed are they which go around in circles, as they shall be called the big wheels".

But what I really appreciate about the Detroit bad boy is under that preening, posturing exterior beats the heart of a genuinely good person. Do a Google search of his encounters with Downs kids, and I think you'll be blown away; there is so much good in the worst of us, and so much bad in the best of us, that it doesn't warrant looking for the fault in any of us.

So in honor of Charlie Bravo Day, I'll leave you with my version of a Kid Rock ballad...

Hit it, boys!

I was left in a crate, but now I'm free
Living it large is my le-ga-cy
I sleep where I want, sloppy drool I give
others do my bidding, I'll let them live,
I like Alpo, Old Roy, and Gravy Train
Whatever dad is eating is what I crave
Toilet water is a special treat,
Hemp flavored dog treats just can't be beat,beat,beat,beat...

Wellllll...
Hey, hey,
I'm the Charlie, I'm the lady in black
Lift your paws in the air, let me see where you're at
I said HEY, HEY,
(Let me see where you're at)
I said HEY, HEY,
(My back needs a scratch)
Head out the window, breeze in my face
Rolling with the inmates I rock this place
Miss Ellie's my home girl, she's all the rave
But the back of the bike is what I crave
I'm back in black, I'm nationwide
Dad's pride and joy, I'm bonafide
I like flouncing with Echo, and Mia too
Take a tinkle in the yard and a big doo doo doo doo doo...
Heyyyyy....
Hey, hey,
I'm the Charlie, I'm the lady in black
Lift your paws in the air, let me see where you're at
I said HEY, HEY,
(Let me see where you're at)
I said HEY, HEY,
(My back needs a scratch, scratch, scratch...)

Charlie: The Clarion Cry of the Lonesome Chark

Approximately 0300 hours this morning, mom arose, purportedly to let Mia and I do our "bidness", but somehow, we instead found ourselves incarcerated in the north wing of the Casa del Whackos, i.e. the dog yard. This will NOT do: I have been way too diligent for way too long on my fight to establish my territory on the bed to allow a setback like this to occur, so I did what I had to do.

From the trumpets of Joshua used to jolt Jericho to the air raid sirens of Great Britain announcing another long night of bombardment, loud noises have been employed to express alarm and call for assistance, and my voice is no different. I began my verbal assault beginning with a few peremptory salvos consisting of yips and whines directed towards the walls of the Casa which escalated quickly into a full barrage of barks, howls, and ultimately, the nuclear option, the MOAB, the Mother of all Bombs if you will, known to military historians the world over as:

The Chark.

Dad had no choice but to immediately capitulate and humble himself by enacting the dreaded Walk of Barefoot Pre-dawn Shame across the dewy wasteland to offer terms of abject surrender, which I graciously accepted. Let it be noted that the instigator of these hostilities (mom) was not in attendance at this ceremony, an issue to be addressed at a later date.

So here I am, once again firmly established in my rightful place on the bed; as set forth in the details of the peace accord, mom has been exiled to the territory of the couch and dad is back in his allotted space at the edge of the world, clutching the edge of the bed with his butt cheeks in a effort to not plunge into the abyss. Max E. Million has used the recent hostilities as an opportunity to increase his own empire, but as discretion is the better part of valor, I have decided to be magnanimous and let things stay as they are for the time being. Besides, that pocket-sized dictator has been known to possess some serious firepower in those hirsute little jaws of his, and I prefer my shiny black hide to continue on in the manner it currently exists:

Unperforated.

So, beyond its obvious use as a weapon of mass destruction, what is the purpose of "The Chark?" It can serve as a reminder that, as I did, we all tend to exist in some form of a crate and only by helping others leave theirs can we hope to escape ours. It can also act as a call to action, a reminder that just because you can't fix it all doesn't mean that you refuse to fix anything; get involved, as there IS life outside of the TV set. It can also provide a wall of sound, drowning out the flood of negativity and bad news created by those that would have you believe that you don't matter and your actions don't make a difference. If a scabby, scaly, starving dog incarcerated in a crate can become an elemental force of nature, just imagine what you can do, right here, right now, with the arsenal of talent you currently have in your possession.

Charlie: Here We Go Again!

I'd better grab the opportunity to post when I can. Traveling with dad is an "unique" experience, and not for everyone; even the patience of mom is tested to the maximum, as he tends to start a trip like the whips of Satan's imps are driving him across the plains. Max and I are cool with it, as it usually means more opportunities to meet and hang out with like-minded travelers at our non-existent destinations, and today was no exception.

We finally stopped in Hinton, OK, where dad met a fledgling small-town pastor having dinner with his beautiful family; this man was free with the information that he was a recovering addict. When dad asked him what he considered his biggest challenge in this new endeavor, the man surprisingly answered:

"My pride"; with a vision such as his, I predict he will go far.

On the way back to the freeway, we spotted two loaded down BMW motorcycles parked at a seedy hotel dad had frequented on past trips; normal people don't just stop and bang on stranger's doors, but dad's lack of "normalcy" has been established long ago. The bikes belonged to a dynamic duo of grandparents in the middle of a month-long journey from California to Kentucky, and who's past trips had included a visit to Tierra del Fuego and trip through Mexico that didn't end so well. That trip came to a sudden halt, as did the man's bike and the life of the cow that wandered into his path in Baja, leaving him (the rider, not the cow) incapacitated for over a year. But past performance is not indicative of future results, and now they're back on the road again.

Max and I used these two lengthy encounters to discover and devour one of the bags of the jerky the Deb sent us, with the expected gastric results; now the interior of the car is heavy with the essence of oily zephyrs and the gurgling of hairy bellies.

At least that's dad's story, as I do recall him having a mocha frappe earlier in the day, and those things are like drinking frozen Drano, only slightly more toxic, er, tasty. Max also had a taste, as evidenced still by the stiffness of his chocolatey-smelling mustache.

See, I told you traveling with the inmates isn't for everyone…

See you on the road!

Dad: Keep Rolling

Dad here; the heat and friction of the sandstone in Moab took its toll on Charlie's getupandgo, and today she's moving around like an old woman. She is digging the attention that mom is lavishing upon her, but personally, I think that she's being a bit overly dramatic. In her mind, she's shuffling around Colorado with a quad cane and orthopedic slippers (Charlie, not mom).

On the other hand, Max has dropped his grumpy Winston Churchill persona and is totally in his element.

There are tradeoffs in everything; while the cloud cover kept the temperature in the sandstone desert to a bearable level, it also negatively affected the ability to frame Moab's magnificent arches against Utah's usually azure skies, and that same sky has dogged us back into Colorado. After such an auspicious beginning, it's sometimes difficult to remember that journeys are a mirror of life, some cycles being indescribably good being offset by periods that just don't seem to "click".

So, what do you do? You have no choice, you keep rolling. If you do feel that you need to pause and reconsider your direction, that's to be expected, but only with the intention of putting the vehicle back in drive as quickly as possible. A motorcycle/house/car/person left sitting idle tends to deteriorate at a much quicker pace than one that's active, and the same is true of our dreams; keep driving.

It's been a fantastic trip so far, as usual, with the people making the difference. Charlie's diplomatic tongue can do more to further her message with one slimy swipe than she can do with a thousand posts. We have encountered people from around the world, Belgium, Holland, Germany, Japan, etc, that have heard Charlie's story and decide to bend down for a pat, only to feel the wrath of an anteater-like tongue, if an anteater's was also a foot wide and covered with gallons of slobber. Max is also incredibly effective in this area, but instead uses his radar like eyebrows and ears to transmit his own peculiar frequency.

And in an open note to Darling Nikki who is fighting cancer back on the east coast; keep driving. I know words seem empty at a time like this, but thoughts and prayers are not; your determination is an inspiration to the whole Las Familia de la Casa del Whackos. As in Charlie's story, it's easy for some to stand by and do nothing when they realize that they can't fix everything, but all you have to do is speak the word and we will do what we can to ease your suffering, financially, spiritually, etc; "service every need as it arises and we will find our ministry". They say that when you laugh, the world laughs with you, but when you cry, you cry alone; I assure you that in the case of the inmates at the Casa, this is not true.

Even though we're all thousands, some even ten thousand miles apart, we all stand together; we be of one blood, ye and I.

Charlie: I'm Sorry, So Sorry

I have a horrible confession to make; sometimes we do things while away from the Casa that we would never even consider doing back home. The allure of new places and experiences, no access to social media, limited oxygen to the brain, fatigue, white line fever, sensory overload, all of these stimuli combine with the catalyst that is the anonymity of the open road to cause some things to "just happen". Trust painstakingly established over the years can be wiped away in a microsecond with one such "indiscretion", then come the uncomfortable silences and averted glances.

The Good Book says "the heart is desperately wicked, who can know it?", and that "pride goeth before a fall"; that it can happen to the best of us must be true, because it happened to me. I failed; I was weighed in the balance and found wanting.

But there are always two sides to any infidelity, and dad carries some blame as well. In this case, dad drove me to it, as odd as that may seem, but there's only so much pressure a girl can take before committing the unpardonable sin, until last night, I fell into temptation.

I slept with mom.

I know, I know, it just "happened"; I was slightly inebriated from the mountain air, my feet were worn sore from the trail, and mom just knew how to push the right buttons. Max had already taken up residence in dad's sleeping bag, a fact that wouldn't have affected matters in the least back at the Casa as I would have rousted him out with a flip of my snout, but this time was different, and I failed. Now I'm paying the price as I gaze across the tent to the distant lump of snoring nylon that marks my erstwhile homeland, and wonder quietly to myself:

Can I ever go home? Will it ever be the same?

Who am I kidding? I got this; we all know that dad's a notorious pushover, just a big pansy, if a 5'6" pansy can be considered "big". I'll just lay a little Charlie tongue lovin's on his face and he'll fold up like a cheap suitcase like he always does.

But the crawl of shame will have to wait; although New Mexico has perfected their sunrises and sunsets, they have yet to work the kinks out of their climate control system, and the frigid morning air is going to postpone my advances until weather conditions are more conducive to groveling.

Besides, Mom had the thermostat at in her sleeping bag set on "just right", and you don't improve on perfection!

Charlie: Hanging Memories on Each Highline Pole

We should have made it home by now, but dad seems to have a love/hate relationship with those state signs positioned at every border crossing. He loves the anticipation of seeing them approach through the haze of bug guts on the windshield, but gets a feeling of sickness and dread in the pit of his stomach when one recedes in the rear view mirror; "well, we won't be seeing THAT one again for a while… (heavy sigh)(suppressed sob)".

We had every intention of leaving Raton early yesterday and rolling hard towards the east and the Casa, but the magnetic pull of the Spanish Peaks just to our north was too much for the steel of dad's wanderlust, and we once again found ourselves passing a rustic "Colorful Colorado" portal. Dad's obviously flawed reasoning was to poke around a bit in the high country before bending it left around noon, which would make the final day on the road a relatively easy one: even from the back seat I could literally hear mom's eyes rolling back in her head like the apples and oranges on a one-armed bandit, although dad would have to find his own jackpot.

Just like the rest of the trip, the details of this particular day are way too varied to fit into this particular blog and will have to somehow be worked into future posts. Suffice to say that at the appointed hour of departure, we instead found ourselves on a high mountain trail at 11,500', with a storm bearing in from the north. The temps plummeted and the clouds rolled in so quickly that visibility dropped to mere feet within minutes, just perfect for concealing any predators, imaginary or otherwise, in the swirling mist. This cover was also instrumental in obscuring from mom the fact that Max was indulging freely in his particular affinity for marmot poop, a fact that would come back to haunt us later in the story.

Then down, down, down, like a trickle transforming into a river as it descends, the trail gave way to a dirt road, then the dirt transformed into asphalt, the two-lane transformed into interstate and the ubiquitous yellow "New Mexico, Land of Enchantment" sign, with its perky red and yellow peppers.

In an unsuccessful attempt to make up for lost time, we rolled long and hard, the gathering darkness to the east concealing predators of a different kind, the black and white patrol cars of the first the Texas, then Oklahoma, State Police. They possess a particular force known to dad as "Pucker Power", or "Mobile Reality"; that the mere sight of a government agency vehicle can provoke such a feeling of guilt in an otherwise innocent person is a post for another day. "To protect and to serve" is a lovely sentiment, but "We'll leave you alone until you actually warrant otherwise" is much preferable. Tired, smelly, and cranky, we finally decided to shut it down for the night and were looking for a suitable bivouac when we hear a liquid "YAAAARCH" from the back seat, followed by a stench that can only be described as "the armpit of Satan".

Remember the marmot poop?

It obviously had been fermenting in Max's reactor core across four states, two-time zones and multiple elevation changes, only to go into meltdown when mom and dad were least equipped to deal with it. Hazmat teams were scrambled from the surrounding states, blankets and towels were burned, and, for once, I stayed out of the way.

Now, it's morning, and the sun is glinting off our fine collection of petrified insects as we speed, er, advance with alacrity, towards the east and home: I feel very confident that you could start a small entomology museum with the specimens embedded in our grill.

Next stop, the Casa.

(Had I known then what I know now, I would have stayed in New Mexico-Dad)

Dad: Deeep Breath; or, How I was Driven Home in my own Crate

The story of Charlie and the story of the crate are inextricably linked; no crate, no Charlie, no story, as horrible as that may sound. It wasn't until she was freed from that stinking, vile, situation that she could become the vibrant, shining, flouncing gooberhead that she is today. Every time that Charlie writes about the importance of leaving your crate, I've personally feel like the biggest hypocrite on the face of the planet. My crate in this particular case was my job of 21 years, and the lock was my company car and four weeks of vacation. I don't mean to discount these things, as they were blessings from God and vital to the story of Charlie: if I hadn't been looking for another way into the office to avoid highway construction I wouldn't have discovered the back roads where I later found Charlie. And if I hadn't had access to the car and vacation time, I couldn't have been able to make the trips to rehome Dash and still take Charlie west, and on and on.

So yesterday, I was involuntarily freed from my crate. Check that; what makes the story even better is, that, on the day of my 21st employment anniversary, I had my nose rubbed in my own poop, was swatted on the nose with a rolled-up newspaper, then was driven home and unceremoniously dumped into my own driveway. As I watched the tail lights of my former crate narrow and recede into the distance, I could hear the CHARK! from the back yard:

"Yo, dad! Are you coming back here to let me out or what?"

This is not to garner sympathy for myself, as I know that those of you in far worse situations. I don't mean to even insinuate that my situation is bad; to the contrary, this is an incredible opportunity. Neither is it meant to generate ill will towards my former employer; for even though the last two decades they have been a great company to be a part of, recent events have forced them to make decisions based on fear. Any decision based solely on fear is always the wrong decision, and the sense of elation I know feel is akin to a boot being lifted from my neck.

But it matters not; that was then, this is now, and now is time for the next chapter.

In case you're wondering, mom has seen the effects of the last few years and also thinks that this can only be for the best, and we all know, momma knows best. Her response to the news when she realized the reason for the car missing from the driveway?

"Thank God!!!"

Will it involve change? Most assuredly. Any idea where those changes may take us? No idea, but as you all know, it's always a party at the Casa, and you're all invited along for the ride.

Now get off of the bed, Charlie, we have things to do!

Charlie: Dockers or Shackles?

What a week; return from a whirlwind trip out west, and Monday dad returned to the daily grind to only find that someone pulled the plug on the grinder, and that was the last time I've seen him dress in his usual emasculating ensemble insipidly described as "business casual". One day of Levi's, since then it's been Wranglers.

For the last twenty-one years, golf shirts and khakis (honey, do these pants make my butt look big? Of course they do, they're PLEATED DOCKERS!) with the ubiquitous laminated identity badge (security? Really? What's at risk here, scratch pads and ink pens?) have been the approved uniform of Those That Make the Rules.

Well, that ship has sailed, that train has left the station, that paste has left the tube, that poop has left the… well, you're getting the picture. When Zach was going to prom, he was considering a flashy tuxedo, when dad had only one question to consider:

What would Dean Martin do?

I'm not suggesting that tuxes should be daily business attire, but what happened to men dressing like men and not sartorial little boys? Since when did baggy shorts, blousy button downs and sandals become acceptable attire for anywhere besides Maui?

Or on the other hand, can you see Mike Rowe showing up for Dirty Jobs wearing Dockers and wing tips? He's a class act but knows that there is a time and a place for everything except for the unholy combination of "business" and "casual". Even Yoda, with his wardrobe consisting of one moldy gray robe, knew that "do or do not, there are no Dockers".

Clothes, car, compensation, all these crates are now gone, but now comes the dreaded duo of complacency and procrastination. Like finding my crate that day on January, this situation must also be viewed as what it is, a great gift not to be squandered, so it's onward and upward.

But it's also an opportunity to spend more time with me, as it IS officially Charlie Bravo Day. I am currently bringing in my best lobbyists to float the idea that every day should be CBD, but I am getting some blow back from Max's side of the aisle, that hairy little partisan; I'll settle HIS hash at the next committee meeting...

Thus Quoth the Charlie

Once upon a midnight dreary, I tossed and turned, all weak and weary
Banished from the bed onto the hardwood floor
When deep beneath the quilts I heard a yarking
A heaving sound, a silent barking
Is it a false alarm, or cause to flee these shores?
Thus quoth the Charlie;
Nevermore.

I dared not peek beneath the covers
As odors abiding there are known to hover
The ghosts of Alpo past, a foul vapour
the inky darkness keeps me from peering

What my foot may touch is what I'm fearing
Should I procrastinate or levitate towards the door?
Thus quoth the Charlie:
Nevermore

Then another issue rears it head
When I spy a spectre from the bed
Upon the wall the silhouette of a dinosaur

Illuminated by the cell phone light
My meager hair rising with fright
O fearless dog, arise and cease thy snores!
Thus quoth the Charlie
Nevermore.

As it turns out, my fears were moot
the yarking sound, it bore no fruit
The odors that I loathe were gone forevermore
The sinister shape filling me with dread
Were the size and shape of Charlie's head
Was there ever any real danger to ignore?
Thus quoth the Charlie:
Nevermore.

And this is true of most our fears
What we can't see consumes our years
That what we dread compares not to what's in store
Shake and stretch, turn on the light
What's wrong is wrong, but there's much more right
O Charlie girl, are there horizons we can't explore?
Thus quoth the Charlie;
Nevermore.

Max: All Quiet along The Western Front

Max here: Pre-dawn at the Casa… if the bed was North America, dad would be sleeping along the coasts of Washington, Oregon and a bit of northern California, with Charlie occupying Nevada, Utah, Idaho, Colorado, Wyoming, Montana, Kansas, Oklahoma, Missouri, Arkansas, Iowa, and the Dakotas. Mia has annexed the rest of southern California from LA down to Tijuana, and I migrate at will like a hirsute band of gypsies from region to region as the mood strikes me.

As this leaves mom with the rest of the continent to occupy as she sees fit, you would think that she would be satisfied with this arrangement, but Charlie continues to expand her territory both east and west; you would think that she would be satisfied with the status quo, but what megalomaniac ever truly finished conquering? Stalin, Hitler, Genghis, Caesar, Alexander, Kanye, all driven by a blind lust and greed, but are nothing compared to the drive and determination of Charlemagne Bravissimo.

But, for now, a tentative armistice had been achieved and all is quiet on the western front, when…

POPOPOPOPOPOP!!!

Shots ring out! Is this another assassination attempt on the Max E Million? Or another failed drive-by perpetrated by the dachshunds down the street? It matters not! Rise and fight! Sound the alarm to marshal our forces to defend the borders of the fatherland! Continue sounding the alarm until, well, until dad issues the decree to terminate the racket with extreme prejudice!

As it turns out, those weren't shots fired: who needs an alarm clock when you have a Charlie shaking her head, popping her ears and jowls like so many floppy black bull whips?

The crisis has passed, but now the resulting adrenaline surge has everyone else at the Casa up and hyperactive...
...except Charlie, who is sprawled out under the covers, sleeping the sleep of the unrepentant.
It's great to be Queen!

Charlie: The Sound

Dad and I have never liked spending much time dwelling on my condition when I exited the crate; it seems that there is more than enough negative garbage being spewed by the media without any help from us. Instead, it has been our mission from the beginning to spread good news, because at the end of the day, there is no bad news, just varying degrees of good news, based totally on our perception.

But sometimes you have to remember where you've been to appreciate where you are, and, more importantly, where you're going. Dad had to take a trip last weekend without me (for which he will pay, I assure you, as I am the Dark Mistress of Guilt), so I took up residence in Kat's futon for the night. At my request, she took the above picture and sent it to dad (the first phase of the guilt attack!).

In times of stress, it seems I always revert to my previous habit of preparing to sleep by first curling my feet under me, conforming myself perfectly to fit the confines of the crate. As I relax, I then spread slowly across the bed like a hairy black octopus, or more appropriately, a encroaching lava flow engulfing everything in my path.

It's important to note that this doesn't happen when I'm feeling cocky and rambunctious, the vast majority of the time, but only during those dark episodes when I find myself lost in doubt. It's then that I have to remind myself of what no longer confines me, of what I have been delivered from, and before you know it, I hear "the sound" that lets me know that all is again right with the world.

What is "The Sound"? For me, it's the bark of the bike as it pulls back into the driveway of the Casa. For dad, it's the CHARK of the Lonesome Charlie, like the mournful wail of a distant lighthouse directing the ship to safe harbor. Your sound is no doubt different, but I assure you that you have one, a clarion reminder of good times in the past and a forecaster of better times in the future. Regardless of how bleak things may seem, nothing is as bad as worrying about it; your own miracle will arrive on due season, but until then, strive to be someone else's. At the least, it helps pass the time, and at the best, you are fulfilling your ministry.
Yo, dad! You got the coffee ready yet? We gots to GO!

Charlie: Enough Already!

Unemployment, social division, an election resembling a uncivil war, bad news permeating the very atmosphere in which we live, a toxic stew every bit as vile as the crate from whence I came; it's sometimes difficult for this normally vivacious girl to maintain a positive outlook and post accordingly.

But then I remember that we all have a mission, and mine has always been to focus on the positive; what kind of ambassador for good would I be if forsook my post just when it is needed most?

Dad's favorite line in "The Last of the Mohicans" comes when Magua(the vengeful antagonist) seeks permission to burn the English prisoners alive in retribution for past injustices; the chief's response to this request: "Magua's heart is twisted, and he would make others into what twisted him".

This is where the majority of our nation is currently at, so twisted with hate and righteous indignation that we are willing to burn our fellow man in the fires of public discourse.

Well, I art the Charles, and I refuse to strike the match. I know that there are both Republicrats and Demoplicans in this family, and we will eventually have to put this whole sorry mess behind us and get back to the business at hand: spreading the message of the Crate. In this case, the crate is our belief that only our chosen candidate can positively affect change, and that the "other guy" is sending us straight into the abyss. Have we no faith?

Haven't bad situations time and again always proven to somehow "work out"?

Things may appear hopeless, but not as hopeless as I felt standing in my own feces in that claustrophobic crate for only God knows how long. But I held on, and an answer arrived, as it surely will in this instance as well. Until then I'm going to continue flouncing through life, dealing with what situations I can affect, peeing on those that I cannot, but always remembering a valuable lesson learned at Max's expense on our last trip out west:

Never hike your leg on a cactus, or squat over a prickly pear; a couple of self-important nimrods arguing in front of teleprompters will be the LAST thing on your mind!

Charlie: Bravissimo Rhapsody

Last Saturday, Miss Ellie took dad and I waaaaay up into the Ozarks to an ADV motorcycle rally; I'm pretty sure that this was the first time that dad went to a motorcycle event in a 31-year-old car with a rowdy dog in attendance, but such is the powers of guilt that I wield.
We decided to test Miss Ellie's 4WD capabilities by camping atop Pilot Knob, the site of an old fire tower, but quickly decided that the old girl is better suited for cruising old back roads than scrambling up steep rock ledges. So instead we set up camp at the base of the climb, still high enough to witness an incredible sunset, though not as high as we had initially wanted.
The sun filtering through the leaves turned them a brilliant shade of gold that could rival the aspens of Colorado, and

the pink and purple skies were reminiscent of New Mexico; although nothing can compare to a Taos sunset, this one was close. I love the Natural State, but there's something altogether different about the Land of Enchantment.

I had initially planned to do some writing, but dad broke out the sleeping bag and I decided instead to lay claim to my particular sleeping spot, which is wherever I decide it is at any given moment. Although the back of the Subaru was comfy, sleep was long in coming as the gears in my brain were still grinding, so I decided to recreate my story, pre-crate even, to the tune of "Bohemian Rhapsody"; why you ask?
Because I am the real Queen! Think about it; we both have great voices and love to delight the masses by cavorting around on stage. Freddie Mercury was limited to playing stadiums and arenas, but all the world is mine!
So here goes…

OK, Max, you count it down… a one and a two and

A basket of ten pups
Quite a large family
The runt of the litter
My childhood a calamity
My mom I surmise
Didn't care that much for me…

I'm just a poor pup
At the base of the hierarchy
it was easy come, easy go

Siblings adopted out, to fates unknown
One by one they vanished, leaving just one waiting;
Just me...
(Piano)

Abandoned, on a county road
they hear my howls as they depart
It's obvious they have no heart
But it's too late, the car is gone
The only thing that's been thrown away is me
Abandoned, oooo-oh oooo
I don't want to starve
But If they're not back again this time tomorrow
I'll carry on, carry on
Because I know I matter.

How much time passed, I'll never know
Standing hunched breaking my back
Ankle deep in my own crap
Oh how I raged, the crate kept me caged
I still refuse to stop and face the truth
Mama, ooo-oh-ooo
Though I refuse to die
I sometimes wish I'd never been born at all
(Guitar)

(Piano, staccato)
I hear a pair of bikes, approaching in the distance
Hondas! Hondas! Carving up the corners!

First they are not stopping, then the exhausts
they start a popping, for me!
Galileo, Galileo,
Galileo, Galileo,
Galileo Figaro – magnifico!
But I'm just a poor dog and nobody loves me (she's
just a poor dog from a large family)
Cast open the crate, this monstrosity!
Easy come easy go (will you let me go)
Where will you stay? (we will not let you go)- let
me go
Who'll pay to spay? (We will not let you go)- let me
go
There's no possible way! (We will not let you go) let
me go
Will not let you go let me go (never)
Never let you go let me go
Never let me go ooo
No, no, no, no, no, no, no!
Oh mama mia, mama mia, mama mia let me go
The Casa del Whackos has put aside a place for me
For me
For me
(All guitars: crescen... er, vibrato... eh, whatever;
crank the amps to 11 and twist the knobs off...)
So they thought they could desert and leave me to
die?
Do they now see that I don't just live but thrive?

Oh, lady, can't do this to a lady
Just had to get free, no crate's stopping me
I'm Charlie.
(Guitars continue)
(Piano, softly)
Everybody matters
It applies to you and me
Everybody matters
I'm Charlie....
(Anyway the wind blows...)
(Gong...})

Charlie: Operation Rise and Shine

Psst! Max! You awake?

(From underneath the covers) I am now, you hyperactive doofus! What do you want now?

As soon as dad wakes up, let's begin bombarding him with guilt so he will feel obligated to take us for a ride!

But what if he has other things he would rather do? Wait a minute, I think I just had a twinge of conscience(shudder)... your Honor, please strike that last comment from the record.

That's more like it, so here's the plan: first, we stare intently at the side of his head until he feels our laser like gaze boring into his consciousness. If that doesn't work I'll start scratching my ear with extreme prejudice, causing my collar to jangle like the Bells of St Mary's, finishing with a violent shaking of the head, popping my ears like two velvety black bullwhips.

Oooo, I like it, no one can sleep through THAT! Then, when I sense a disturbance in the force, I will take up my position on his chest and breathe into his nostrils the breath of life, or at the very least the aroma of my loins, as I have just engaged in my practice of daily vigorous hygiene.
I love it when a plan comes together; as soon as he reluctantly emerges and starts rummaging through his drawers for a pair of drawers, begin cavorting about like absolute lunatics. I'll start dashing madly around the room, making sure that my horny hooves cause as much damage to the tops of dad's hairy little hobbit feet, while you lay on your back and thrash, snort, contort and generally convince him that you've lost your mind.

What about Mia?

Oh, you don't you worry about her; she's outside getting her feet good and soaked with the morning dew, and will no doubt rise to the occasion once Mom let's her back in. OK, Charlie, Dad looks good and relaxed, so let's get this party started! Operation Rise and Shine commencing in 5, 4, 3, 2….

Uh, wait just a second, Max; off the record, have you ever had gas so bad that it sounded (and felt) like your butt cheeks had been Tasered?

No, why would you bring that up at a time like this?

Oh, no reason; carry on.

Charlie: The Best of Times

Life at the Casa is strange; last night I had exhausted myself by barking at the trick or treaters and had crashed on the living room floor. Mia sauntered into the room and I awoke to find a red dog casually hunching on my head as if this is perfectly acceptable behavior, which it is not. I arose with alacrity to return the favor, while Max looked on from the relative safety of the couch, and dad tried to studiously ignore the debauchery occurring scant feet away, until Mom entered the room and order was restored.

The ancient Chinese had a curse: "may you live in interesting times", but Charles Dickens probably summed it up best, "It was the best of times, it was the worst of times, it was the age of wisdom, it was the age of foolishness, it was the epoch of belief, it was the epoch of incredulity, it was the season of Light, it was the season of Darkness, it was the spring of hope, it was the winter of despair.

Emergency surgeries, major life changes, job loss, etc; if anyone had been on the outside looking in for the last few years, they would no doubt classify this era as "the worst of times" at the Casa del Whackos, but this is not the case. Dad and I were thinking of the good things that have also occurred lately, events so incredible that they can't be defined or explained, so I won't even try. Some have burned brightly only to seemingly flicker out and die, others are just beginning to smolder, but I believe all will bear fruit in due season.

In our country and in our lives, it's very difficult to accept that there are no "good" and "bad" times, but only varying degrees of "good", based on our perception. Imagine circumstances where the economy is causing a large corporation to quake, but during this time, a lowly worker at the bottom of the hierarchy celebrates the birth of a long-sought-after child; the corner office executive would no doubt describe it as the worst of times, while the receiving clerk in the basement would have a totally different viewpoint.

Or the case of the Casa; it's always fantastic to liberated from your crate, but sometimes daunting to determine which direction to go to avoid being trapped in another. All I know is that one has to keep moving; if a Big Fish doesn't keep water moving over its gills, it will drown in the very water meant to sustain it.

The point of all this? Don't know that I have one in particular, except to keep us all conscious of the importance of movement; you can't come through difficult times if you're standing still.
There's always plenty of movement at the Casa!

Charlie: Vacilando, PT II

Hey, dad!

'Sup, Charlie?
Whatcha doin'? It doesn't appear to be very dog inclusive, at least from where I'm sitting.

Don't play dumb, you self-centered diva. You know good and well that I'm dealing with the carnage that you inmates leave in the garage; to get this level of destruction, I almost suspect you of bussing dogs in from neighboring cities to participate in your protests.

Well dad, isn't it true that "black labs matter", as do all dogs regardless of level of pigmentation?

Now, Charlie, no need to try to get me discombobulated by getting all philosophical this early in the morning, it's bad enough like it is without being humbled by a creature that nibbles her butt in mixed company. And by the way, I'm perfectly aware of where your sitting; just because I reposition a motorcycle does not equate to an open invitation to hop up and go for a ride.

Well, dad, the investment commercials state that "past results do not indicate future performance", but at least in your case, I know this to be false. As always, I will continue to bombard you with guilt rays from my perch high atop Mt Suzuki, and as always, you will eventually crumble beneath my superior will and intellect. I can wait you out, as I have all the time in the world... or do I?
(Guilt Ray being loaded into the firing chamber, launching in 3,2,1... weapon away)

As you are aware, dad, dogs have significantly shorter lifespans than humans, so you should always take full advantage of any opportunity for interaction. And the life you save may be your own, as studies show that time spent with a dog lowers stress, increases testosterone, shrinks belly fat, and improves chronic halitosis.

All right, Charlie, I can see where this is going to end up, so if you'll stop that insane charking, we'll head out for a bit. You do know that Mom is going to be a bit "perturbed", to say the least. Any ideas as to an actual destination?

Well, John Steinbeck used a Spanish word, "vacilando", to describe the travels with his Charlie. There is no English translation, but it simply means a journey without a set destination, not just wandering aimlessly but always searching. So even though we can't take off for points and parts unknown, what say that we go vacilando for just a little bit? May not be the best, but it will do until the best presents itself...
(Dad's such a pushover...)

Charlie: Thanksgiving

Unbeknownst to either of us, two years ago today two separate tragedies were working to bring dad and I together; mine was occurring due to a lifetime spent in the crate, and dad's was stealthily advancing on two wheels.

Many have asked about my life BC (before Casa), but truthfully, I remember very little of my time before the crate. They say that sometimes an event can be so traumatic that your mind will erase any solid memory of that particular time, but I really don't think that is the issue in my case; I think that I am so fixated on milking every molecule out "here and now" that I don't have time to ever fret about the "that was then". If anything, my former condition only serves as a vague backdrop to highlight what I am now; an elemental force of nature, a power source without a dimmer switch. There is no halfway status with this girl; I now flounce, sleep, eat, love, lick, with total abandon, at that even extends to the baser functions. If my name wasn't already Charlie Bravo, and I was a applicable plumbing, I would name myself I.P. Freely, as I have absolutely no shame; life is way too short for such meaningless inhibitions.

So, what am I thankful for this year? This post would go on for days if I listed everything, but as anyone who has ever had a life altering connection can understand, the first thing is Dad. The only way I can truly comprehend a human's relationship with this concept of "God" is to equate how a rescue dog feels about her savior. And if Heaven is what I experience when I'm close to dad, then what is Hell but a separation from the same? Even the agnostic Dante believed that hell was simply a separation from God, as what pain could be worse?

Pretty heavy dogma to be charking on Thanksgiving Eve, so I'll move on; I'm also thankful for you, the lifeblood that keeps my story alive. Without an audience, music is just molecules of air bumping together, and without readers, writing is just a collection of marks marring a page. Even more special are the relationships formed over the last two years; I don't want to mention names as I'm sure I would leave someone out, but you know who to you are. We may never actually meet on this side of the Great Divide, but it doesn't really matter; the world is a better place just knowing some people are in it.

This reminds me of an elderly lady that dad once visited in the hospital; it was obvious that she probably wasn't going to make it through the night and both struggled with small talk to fill the void. As he was leaving, she stopped him in his tracks when she matter-of-factly said,
"See you on the other side; but we won't be brother and sister over there"
As you can imagine, Dad's mind was thoroughly blown, but before he could ask the meaning of such a statement, she finished with...

"Over there, we'll be as one".

Happy Thanksgiving from the Casa del Whackos; we be of one blood, ye and I.

Dad: The Life You Save May Be Your Own

Charlie's out like a light from an apparent tryptophan overdose. Before anyone starts freaking out and turns me into the ASPCA, tryptophan is the ingredient in turkey that causes drowsiness, and it appears that the Charles is remarkably susceptible to its properties.

As promised, here's the story of the accident that ultimately led us to Charlie. It's a long tale, with many twists and turns, but bear with me; a lot of of miracles happened in a very short time to bring us to where we are today.

Zach and I ride what is commonly known as dual sport motorcycles, or adventure bikes; street legal motorcycles that are also dirt worthy. ADV riders are notorious for loading their bikes down with camping gear and taking them into desolate places under all kind of extreme conditions. If this group of misfits could explain why they do what they do, they probably would quit doing it, but it gets in your blood; a trip across the state becomes a trek across the country, and if you're incredibly lucky, eventually around the world.

The day after Thanksgiving in 2014, we loaded up the bikes and headed west for a short overnighter into the Ouachita mountains; we hooked up with Bryan, a fellow rider we had met in Moab, UT on a previous excursion. After a cold night under the stars, we saddled up for a day of dirt in one of the most remote areas of Arkansas; everything was perfect. The leaves had reached their peak color, the sun rose high in the sky, chasing the chill from the air as we chased each other down dirt roads which eventually gave way to rugged trails. It was on a long downhill section of such a trail that was so much fun that I just HAD to ride back to the top and run it again; Bryan and Zach wisely waited at the bottom. When I didn't arrive in a reasonable amount of time, they knew something was amiss.

This particular trail was laced with water bars, mounds of dirt crossing the trail to control erosion; these also serve as great launching pads for a middle-aged idiot on a DR650. Even though I wasn't going THAT fast, it was on the backside of one of these jumps that my front tire landed in a rut, whipsawing the bike to the left and me to the right and off the bike. I landed abdomen first on a recently sawn stump roughly the size of a paint can; I say "landed", but I actually remember bouncing. I blacked out for a bit, but I think I had recovered enough to sit up by the time Zach got back up the hill to check on me.

The pain was bad, but not debilitating, and as the impact was to the left side of my stomach and away from any vital organs, or so I thought, we elected to press on. I had no idea that the colon descends the left side, and I had ruptured mine, the contents of my bowels turning my insides into a toxic wasteland. The pain began to gradually build until I couldn't even see, let alone pilot a bike, so Bryan turned back to retrieve a trailer while Zach and I tried to make it to where we could at least find a cell signal.

Finally, after approximately three hours, I had to say enough is enough. I didn't want Zach to see me laying on the ground, so I remember slumping over an old split rail fence. The pain was such that I couldn't even focus my eyes on the GPS to find the next town; we knew that Mena, AR lay approximately ten miles to the west and had a small hospital, so Zach had no choice but to leave me and ride cross country in search of help; only then did I slide off the fence onto the ground.

Words cannot describe the feeling of watching my son's tail light vanish into the woods, knowing that it could quite possibly be the last time I saw him, or anyone, for that matter. At the same time, I had the peace of knowing that this wasn't his first rodeo; we had been in some tight spots before and he could keep his cool with the best of them. If there was help to be found, he would find it; he had his job, and I had mine: staying alive until he returned.

I faded in and out of consciousness, then heard people talking; "I think he's drunk!". A group of off road vehicles had become lost and had stumbled across me laying on the ground. One of the riders happened to be an ER nurse out of Ft Smith, and upon hearing my symptoms, had the other riders strip their coats and coveralls to cover me. She then lay down beside me to use her warmth to keep my from going into shock; during one time of consciousness, I remember asking her," I know you know the signs; am I going to make it?" Her response: "I can't say, but if you go out again, I need permission to do what I can to resuscitate you". I'm thinking, "permission? Hell, hook jumper cables to my nipples and shock me back to life if you have to!". On a side note; since that day, I have tried my best to find the name of that lady, or anyone else in her group. I have contacted the area ranger station, the local sheriff, state police, etc, to no avail, and I'm usually pretty effective at finding that type of information; it's like she just vanished. Make of that what you will, but I know what I believe.

Meantime, Zach was making the ride of his life (and mine), and actually found park ranger eight miles away; the ranger had received a snippet of a phone call concerning a rider down in the Ouachitas, but had lost the signal before he could get the particulars of my location.

Zach led him to me, and I awoke to the sight and sound of blue gloved snapping fingers in my face, and a voice saying, "stay with me, now! Don't close your eyes!"

The rest is a pain racked blur; a rumble of a 4wd truck, then the chop of a helicopter, cold air as they wheeled me across the ramp and into the hospital. Someone ripping away at my favorite pair of armored riding pants. Then, buck naked and strapped to an operating table, masked faces and bright lights, then nothing. If this was heaven, I sure didn't want to be here.

To be continued…

Dad: The Life You Save May Be Your Own, Part Deux

"One, two, three; lift!"

Who are these people, and why are they levering me from one bed to another? And why do I have hoses and tubes inserted into every hole I have, and even into a few that someone has taken the liberty to add? And will the indignities never end? It appears that I'm now the proud owner of a shiny new colostomy bag, attached to my gut like some sort of plastic parasite; if someone won't do me a huge favor and just go ahead and shoot me, just give me the gun and I'll do it myself.

I awoke in a level 2 trauma center an hour south of Little Rock; Joann and Alex made it there just as I was coming out of surgery, and Zach made it in from the west with the bikes on Bryan's trailer. I didn't know it at the time, but the waiting room was full of friends and family, with Alex directing traffic like a pint-sized Napoleon. I won't go into all of the gory details, but a few do stand out as particularly memorable. One such was when, in the middle of the night, an older nurse was making rounds; I had been incarcerated for three days at that time, and as a result was akin to Lazarus in the Bible as "I stunketh". The nurse informed me that she was going to give me a bath; when I, shall we say, "expressed my reservations", she told me, "you gots to be gettin over that!". She then stood me up, stripped me down, and gave me a scrubbing that was miraculous, especially considering that she left any hide remaining whatsoever. Actually, it was so heavenly that I told her that whenever I got this plethora of tubes removed, she and I were heading for Vegas. When I informed JoAnn about the encounter the next morning, I was not a little surprised when my wife unreservedly gave her blessing should I ever decide to actually make the trip.

After seven days of such hilarity, they finally sent me home; I could scarcely look at the bag, much less the 9" gaping incision in my gut that had to be repacked twice daily. I have no idea what I would have done if JoAnn hadn't stepped up to the plate; to say it was a depressing time is the understatement of the year. Even under much less trying circumstances, I am not a good patient, and for her to put up with my shenanigans qualifies her for immediate sainthood as far as I'm concerned. It was during this time that the infamous "poop on the foot" episode occurred, a story humbling beyond belief at the time but one of my favorites today, although I still can't believe I still tell it.

So how does all this relate in any way to Charlie? After a few weeks of hiding in a dark house, I had to get out. I had lost so much weight that I could easily hide the bag under my riding gear, so on a cold, rainy day in January, Zach came over and we took the street bikes out for a spin. It was on this ride that we spotted Charlie's crate; to be honest, we didn't stop the first time we passed. We had seen a few rabbit hunters in the area, and at first I put the two together. We then switched bikes and made a second pass; it was then that we saw her emaciated condition, and I flashed back to laying on the ground myself, watching Zach's tail light vanish through the trees. Would we have stopped anyway? Of that I have no doubt, but, by previous experience, we knew that it was "right". As we were both riding Honda CB motorcycles that fateful day, she named herself Charlie Bravo.

The network of ADV riders across the country is notorious for their dog relays, and it was my initial intention to get Charlie stabilized then adopted out to someone suitable. On a side note, Dash/Takoda Steele's dad is one such rider, which is how we both came to drive over a thousand miles each to meet in Raton, NM in the dash for Dash relay, another story for another day.

As we needed another dog at the Casa like I need another hole in my head, or elsewhere, I posted Charlie's story over on ADVrider.com, and, as a result, quickly compiled a list of riders across the country willing to adopt CB. But life is what happens when you're making other plans, and the goofy girl began to successfully insinuate herself as the Queen of the Casa del Whackos.

And here we are today; on one side, a mountain of debt and a gut full of scars, and on the other side, tipping the scales towards the good, a black dog with one heckuva story.

I think it's a pretty fair trade.

Dad: I Didn't Come for the Results, I Came for the Experience

Two years ago today, everything went from good to not so good in a microsecond. Mom questioned the wisdom of me wanting to revisit the scene of my near demise; all I could think of were the ten lepers that were healed by Jesus, and only one returned to offer thanks. As it turned out, this trip wasn't only for me.

Charlie and I loaded up Miss Ellie and headed west for Wolf Pen Gap; the first stop was unplanned, the 4th floor of the hospital in Hot Springs where I had been incarcerated. Seeing the halls where I had made my laps, dragging a mess of wires, tubes and other medical misery in an effort to wake up the plumbing, snapped everything back into focus. I left a note for a particular nurse who had went above and beyond the call of duty, and no, it wasn't the nurse who had performed the sponge bath, but thanks for asking.

Then it was west towards the scene of the crime; it remained overcast and the fog refused to burn off as Ellie chugged through the mountains. After the pavement turned to dirt for what seemed an eternity, there it was; what I remembered as a split rail fence were actually railroad ties bolted together. For a good while, I had the place to myself, the only sound was of Charlie very disrespectfully flouncing through the woods, totally unconcerned about any past experiences, negative or otherwise. Then the sound of four wheelers and ATVs broke the reverie, and like Charlie, it was time to move on.

I remember the ride from the fence to the field where the helicopter could land being the most painful of my life, with every creek crossing and pothole carefully designed to shake my guts out onto the floor of the ambulance. As it turned out, there were no major obstacles of any sort, just a fairly smooth gravel road, although I would have never believed that at the time.

There is absolutely no cell coverage in that area; when Zach rode for help, the only public land line for a 50 miles radius was at the Big Fork Country Store, my next destination. The owner remembered every detail of that day, how she had stayed open for Zach until the helicopter had departed from the field across the highway from her store. She said that the trails of Wolf Pen are littered with crosses, memorials to those who didn't make it out, and of all those that had mishaps like mine and survived, I was the first to return. It was then that I realized that this trip wasn't meant for me.

The next stop was to meet the ranger who Zach had encountered and led to where I lay. His willingness to share his recollections of that day were vital to me being able to put the pieces together, and I had to meet this guy.

He agreed to meet at the station for a quick chat before going back out on patrol, one of his initial comments when I pulled into the parking lot:

"when I saw that old brown Subaru coming up the road, I knew that had to be you".

We had a great time discussing the twists and turns of life, how the accident in Wolf Pen flowed into the story of Charlie; I can't remember the last time I was so impressed with a fellow human being. Humble yet professional, personable yet direct, what a totally class act. I have no idea how, when, or if we will ever cross paths again, but sometimes that's not the issue; the world is a better place just knowing that some people are in it.

I never discovered the name of any in the group that stayed with me until the paramedics arrived; the only witness listed in the ranger's report was Zach. But make no mistake; I'm not finished yet, and someday I will find them.

We rolled hard back to the Casa as we were expecting a special guest, a rider from Cordova, Spain who is riding his Africa Twin motorcycle up, down, and around the world. After spending the night at the Casa, he's continuing across Texas, New Mexico, California, then south to the tip of South America and Tierra del Fuego; I realize that "he that compares himself to others is not wise", but it sure makes my little adventures look paltry in comparison.

Charlie: The Road Always Rises

It's good to be back; I understand why dad felt the need he to post this weekend with it being the anniversary of the bag and all, but really? Sure, he makes a great chauffeur, but he needs to leave the writing to me.
One of the benefits of presiding over the Casa del Whackos is the number of pilgrims we have had the privilege of entertaining, in some ways the descendants of the honorable hobos of yesteryear. Ukraine, Spain, Canada, England, Yanqui, all of them willing to forego the comforts of home for a home on two wheels, at least for a time.

The ranger in Mena expressed disbelief when we told him that we needed to get back to the Casa as we were expecting a traveler from Spain, and it made dad think; why do we trust this type of people?

Dad is no Pollyanna with a saccharine view of society, and we fully realize that there are some bad people out there. First and foremost, people become what you expect of them. Second, this isn't dad's first rodeo, and with age comes experience and a certain level of discernment. Third, he has me; I also have a sixth sense about these things, and I'm capable in my own way of defending the perimeter if necessary.

But we have found that when people are on these types of journeys they are in search of something, especially if they are willing to make themselves vulnerable and forego the comforts of a motel to rely on the kindness of a stranger. Could these encounters go bad? Of course, but so far, they have all been life changing experiences for the good. The hand giving is always higher than the hand receiving, but when all parties involved are willing to give, everybody wins.

Sometimes when a visit comes to an end, you just want to stretch the experience as long as you can. Although yesterday was cold and grey, dad called some local riders to escort Xuankar on his journey. He usually communicates in a language I can understand (dad, not Xuankar), but yesterday he started making these bizarre noises, something about leaving me home because it was too cold, blah, blah, blah; as if THAT was going to happen! I AM the Queen, and with rank cometh privilege, one of which is to overrule dad's bad decisions.

We rolled out of town towards Hot Springs, and somehow this trip became different; I've ridden many miles on the back of the bike, but the key word there is "ridden", looking from side to side, barking at squirrels, you know, the good things in life. Yesterday, something clicked, and instead of randomly looking around, I became actively involved. I would find myself looking over his right shoulder when we would dive deep into a hard right-hander, and the same on the left. We soon developed a rhythm, a synchronicity if you will; no longer just a ride but more of a cooperative dance.

We said our goodbyes and turned towards home, and it made me reflect on the similarities between the ADV riders and the followers of my page; although one group is predominantly male and the other female, and of all nationalities and political beliefs, both are connected by a common cause. Both are well seasoned and have shown a willingness to suffer, and have suffered, for the things they love. But this suffering hasn't turned them bitter but has caused them to embrace even more fiercely the things they love.

In accord with your place on it, the road may be flat and boring or rough and rocky, but it's always rising towards a new horizon, and soon the difficult sections will be a distant memory.
From the family of Charlie Bravo: Godspeed, Xuankar; we be of one blood, ye and I,

Charlie: His talk was worn smooth from use in many places

Of all Disney's seven dwarves, "Bashful" is the one that Dad just doesn't "get". Dopey, Grumpy, Happy, maybe, but Bashful? Not when dad would talk to someone stump if the stump would hold still long enough. Invariably the conversation works around to me and my message, and he feels the need to be very descriptive when relating my my previous condition, not necessarily for the shock factor, but more importantly, to demonstrate how far I've come. Can you imagine how unimpressive it would be if the clouds didn't contrast with the sky?

Then usually the subject changes to how evil people are to do something this horrible, but again, I have to disagree; although it's true that that there are some thoughtless or downright cruel people out there, there are SO many more that tip the balances in the favor of good. Need some evidence? Check out the mettle of the followers of this page, or better yet, go sneak a peak in the mirror, and the resulting good you find will be more than sufficient to overcome a thousand FB news feeds; Madre de Dios, what type of bottom feeders do these people take us for?

So, a little reminder every now and then as to how far I've came, to remind everyone (myself included) that, regardless of how grim and hopeless things may appear, there is always hope. From the confines of the crate to the call of the open road, life is always good, although I will admit sometimes "more good" than others, but when it's GOOD, just freaking WOW! The sunsets over New Mexico? Waterfalls tumbling out of the Ozarks? The perfect song at the perfect time? Puppy breath? Dog farts? I realize that that last one may be a stretch, but think about it; how many clouds of funk would you be willing to endure for just one more day with a special dog?
Go forth today and find the beauty, and if it's difficult to find, go create some for somebody else, and I promise you that your own will be revealed to you; it's always a party, so send out some more invitations, and RSVP

Dad: The Next Step

Dad here; facts are like bikinis, as what they reveal is interesting but what they hide is vital. Every time I see the story and pictures of our first meeting with Charlie resurface somewhere new on the Web, I'm struck by the realization that the whole world is seeing a picture of me wearing a colostomy bag and doesn't even know it.

Thankfully, the procedure was able to be reversed after the longest four months of my life. Sometimes these things can't be "taken down"; I'll never forget waking up after the second surgery and not being able to make myself look under the sheet to see if my parasitic plastic buddy still had his adhesive lips had affixed to my abdomen.

Thankfully, all went well, so to speak, but the experience has given me a great appreciation for those that deal with any type of physical or mental adversity; you are true champions.

Last week, Charlie and I reached out to the ranger and other first responders that were involved in initially saving my bacon; I haven't found everyone yet, and I thought that I had exhausted all of my resources when from out of the blue, I received a call from the paramedic that commanded the scene. It is his hand and leg that appear in the picture of me on the ground at the extraction point; file that bit of info away for just a minute.

Out of respect for his privacy, I won't post his name here, but I expect he might when he sees this post; that's his prerogative. We talked for much longer than either of us probably should have; when I mentioned the circumstances behind our discovery of Charlie, the colostomy bag, etc. He told me that he had personally a lost a leg when, as a three-year-old child he had stepped into a hole that happened to be home to a rumba of rattlesnakes and was struck repeatedly before he could pull himself clear; one of the bites was over 1.5" across, and that was just one of many. I can't begin to imagine his anguish or that of his parents, dealing with a child losing a limb, especially in rural Arkansas at that particular time. As a result, he is on his 37th consecutive prosthesis with all the accompanying issues.

Now when I see that picture of my angels gathered around me on the ground, will I see a one-legged man? No, I see a man that overcame incredible adversity and went on with his life, ultimately saving mine.

So, I'm not going to waste it; many decisions must be made, and soon, which will affect the direction of Charlie's story. I am fully aware that we have all been given an incredible opportunity to make a difference; I know the "who", the "why", and even a bit of the "where", but the big question for now is how? And when?
The horizon is limitless; who wants to go for a ride?

Charlie: Blue Charkmas

12:18 AM at the Casa; although the calendar tells me it's officially Charlie Bravo Day, somehow, I just can't seem to make myself believe it. I mean, I AM the Diva dog, and as such, unaccustomed to these vague feelings of self doubt that seem to be stampeding uninvited through my mind. As much as I would like to pretend that this condition doesn't exist, denial is much more than just a river in Egypt but what is the cause? And what is the cure?

Some might say it's just Seasonal Affective Disorder, or SAD, a condition where decreased activity and lack of sunlight seems to take their toll on the psyche; this feeling of malaise is highlighted against a backdrop of sometimes forced gaiety of the "holiday" season. But, for many, this time of year holds as many melancholic as merry memories.

I remember little of my life BC (Before Casa), but it stands to reason that if dad and I found each other in January, I probably spent at least the month of December incarcerated in the crate; this residual feeling of separation could possibly explain the empathy I feel towards those that sometimes struggle with this particular season. But that's the thing about memories, both good and bad: you have to be alive to have them.

One of dad's favorite books is "Cold Mountain" by Charles Frazier; there is a particular passage spoken by the old goat woman that rings particularly true at times such as these:

"That's just pain; it goes eventually. And when it's gone, there's no lasting memory. Not the worst of it anyway. It fades. Our minds aren't made to hold on to the particulars of pain the way we do bliss. It's a gift God gives us, a sign of His care for us.
Besides, you get to be my age, remembering pleasures long ago is painful enough!"

So, if you're currently on the mountain? Celebrate while you're at the apex, and give no thought for the valley to come, for it will surely be followed by another summit, and so the cycle continues; this too shall pass.
And while there may not be a cure for this seasonal malady, there is surely a salve, but that's where this medication differs from most; it is only effective when

administered to a fellow sufferer. Forget the commercialism and focus instead on the real reason for the season and His example of utmost selflessness, and the blahs will surely be banished.

Dad and Max have long since relocated to the couch to escape my tossing and turning, a situation that I must remedy immediately; make no mistake about it, I am STILL the queen!

Dad: Step Back

About the current political/social debacle; The Chinese have a saying, "when it's not necessary to say a thing, it's necessary not to say it". I'll take it a step further; I don't know what to say, but I feel compelled to say it anyway.

We have been on the road for the last few days, with plenty of great stories and experiences to relate, so stay tuned; the story of Emma and the Tunica Humane Society is forthcoming Sunday as promised.

One of the peculiarities of traveling in the temperamental Subaru is that she only has an old push-button AM/FM radio for a would-be sound system; the result is a lot of chasing static from the left to the right of the dial. Even though I try to turn it off and live for the rhythm of the road, I find myself continually returning to the sound of the crime, so you can only imagine the amount of opinionated aural sludge that gets pumped through Miss Ellie's tinny speakers.

So here I am, camping and exploring some of the most beautiful places in all creation, in the company of two of the finest, most loyal traveling companions any man could ask for, and what do I do? I saddle myself with worries and concerns that I couldn't affect one iota if I was home at the Casa, much less out and about.

I know that we are all have our knickers in a twist over the current status of our nation, and the whole world, for that matter. I can only imagine the number of differing viewpoints among the readers of this page, but what I would rather focus on is what brings us together, not what drives us apart. Regardless of our political, religious, or social differences, is gives me an immense deal of gratitude and peace knowing that something as simple as the story of a ragged dog in a crate can bring us all together.

So step back from the maelstrom of the media. Take a deeeeep breath; inhale peace. Exhale hate. As I write these words, the snores of the inmates sprawled everywhere creates a much more satisfying symphony than anything being pumped over the airwaves; they are resting peacefully in the confidence that no matter what anyone one else may say, all things work together for the good.

And now, for some inexplicable reason, Charlie has risen from the dead and has decided that an extended face-licking session is in order, so it looks like we'll be occupied for a while.

Dad: Miss Ellie makes a brake for it

The Chinese have a curse, "may you live in interesting times"; and the last half of 2016 at the Casa has surely been "interesting", much like a train wreck is "interesting". From the beginning, the mission of this page has been to be a non-saccharine refuge from the barrage of negativism on social media. But as with the stories of Stevie's passing, the colostomy saga, the layoff, etc, I have to consider the fact that, as extended family, you deserve to hear the sometimes not-so-pretty backstory, as uncomfortable as it is for me to tell it.

Since the layoff in September, there have been so many minor setbacks pile up at the Casa that you could spin a sitcom out of the situation; car problems, house problems, plumbing problems, then more car problems, etc., etc. Fix one? Two more pop up. And are these "normal" problems, with easily definable solutions? Are you kidding? This IS the Casa, where weirdness abounds.

The latest example:

Miss Ellie is an awesome old car, but she is an old car, with all the accompanying idiosyncrasies that come with age. Mom likes running through the gears of the five speed so she drove the Subie to work at the hospital earlier this week. When she tried to drive home that night, the cantankerous old biddy refused to budge (Miss Ellie, not mom). I was called in to possibly administer first aid; I tried various methods of persuasion, tapping on the calipers, rocking the car back and forth, even giving the car a stern but knowledgeable stare, but nothing would convince the old girl to move. I have since learned that older Subarus have a "hill holder" feature that prevents the car from rolling backwards at a stoplight, and Ellie's had a developed a chronic case of "cableus snapitis", causing the brakes to lock up.

Not knowing this at the time, I had no choice but to leave her in the middle of the deserted parking lot to be dealt with in the light of the next morning, when there were LOTS of passers-by to witness my latest humiliation. The next day, I dropped off mom at work and trudged up the hill to do what must be done, but Miss Ellie was nowhere to be found. Had she tired of life with Charlie and decided to make a break for freedom? Had she been stolen? Who would steal a 30-year-old Subaru, and how much would insurance pay? Had hospital security seen her sitting overnight and had her towed? So many unanswered questions. I was in the process of calling security when I spied Ellie's nose poking sheepishly out of the trees at the edge of the lot: evidently the frozen parking brake problem had somehow miraculously resolved itself during the night, and she had rolled backwards down the hill.

An object in motion tends to remain in motion until acted upon by an outside force, in this case probably a physician's expensive Mercedes, but there was no such Mercedes. There was a curb, a curb separating the parking lot from a very steep hill, a curb that Miss Ellie had decided to jump with her back wheels. With some scrubby pine trees being the only obstacle stopping her from ending up on the interstate far below, this was not going to end well for anyone concerned.

But her front wheels didn't clear the curb, and that's how I found her this morning, hanging by her elbows like "yo, dad! where have YOU been all night?"

Embarrassing? You have no idea. Miraculous? Equally so. But sometimes you have no choice but to laugh and go on. I have to ask myself: As bad as things may seem at times, would I trade my current situation at the Casa for the soul sucking life before the layoff, with the security of a company car, vacation, paycheck, etc?
Not on your life.
I have no idea where this road is going, but I do know that we're in for one hell of a good ride. Traveling without adversity is just touring, and I can't wait to see where journey takes us.

Who wants to ride shotgun?

Tomorrow: how Miss Ellie redeemed herself and saved Christmas.

Twas the Night before Charkmas

Twas the night before Christmas at the Casa del Whackos
Deb, Kathy, and Sandy had sent boxes of snackos
the goodies were stashed well out of harm's way
So ungnawed on 'til Christmas is how they would stay.

Mom was preparing a late midnight snack
For the arrival of Lola, Tara, and Zach
Alex and Echo, from the trip a bit queasy
Presided all over by the Spirit of Stevie

As bedtime approached, the dogs threw a din
Demanding to be let out, and then let back in
When hope appeared lost, to get them to bed
They collapsed where they stood, to sleep like the dead

Then, up on the bed there arose such a scuffle
Dad's covers are gone, he has naught but dust ruffle!
And superhero PJ's to cover his legs
a passel of canines hogging the rest of the bed.

Yo, Maxwell, hey, Mia, show old dad some lovins
If Charlie won't scoot over, there's gonna be shovins!

Then out in the garage there arose such a clatter
 Santa's sleigh threw a rod, extended warranty don't matter
If he's going to finish his deliveries tonight
He'll need a new mode of transport, maybe even dad's bike.

But wait, before you go, at least think this through!
The unanswered question is the old Subaru!
Miss Ellie's an old girl, was never a cutie
She's slow but she's steady, she'll haul plenty of booty!

So Santa, if you must, if this option is last
I request that you at least chip in for the gas
It's not my intention to be such a grouch
Get your own milk and cookies; and wait on the couch.

Dad took the old car instead of the sleigh
Loaded with presents and one stowaway
Charlie saw no need to ask for permission
Couldn't pass such a chance to take such a mission.

Together they traced a path through the skies
On the ultimate road trip to deliver surprise
And high above the Casa was heard a faint bark
Merry Christmas to all, and to all a Good Chark!

Book IV: The Middle Ages

Survey: Should you get a dog?

Dad recently came across an online test to determine if one is ready for pet ownership. I'm a polite dog, so I won't come right out and say that the premise was insanely stupid, but I will insinuate that the author must have eaten paint chips as a child. A few samples of the questions:

We're considering a new pet because:

A. The kids really want a puppy. Me? Not at all.

B. We all love dogs — me included.

C. The kids want a dog, and I'm warming up to the idea.

D. It's a sickness

We are:

A. Homeowners.

B. Renters.

C. Comfortable running an exclusive bed and breakfast for a bunch of hairy little ingrates

If you're still renting, have you checked your lease for breed/size restrictions and any additional fees that may be added to your rent for having a pet?

A. Yes, we're good to go!

B. Yes. There are some restrictions and/or fees, but I'm not worried.

C. Yes. We're not allowed to have a dog, but I plan to anyway.

D. No, maybe I should do that.

E. Deposit? What deposit?

Do you have other pets?

A. Yes, and I'm not sure how they'll handle a dog.

B. Yes, but they've been well-socialized with pets of our friends and family.

C. No, this will be our first.

D. Uh, the term "pets" would insinuate some measure of hierarchy…

You are financially ready to accept ownership of a dog when

A. Your first name is the Donald

B. Your psychic hotline has advised you that multiple trips to the plasma donor center is in your immediate future

C. When one day when you're shooting at some food, up from the ground comes a bubbling crude.

While on vacation, we would:

A. Stay in a pet-friendly hotel and bring the dog along!

B. Have a family member or friend dog sit.

C. Pay to leave the dog with a boarding service.

D. Infuriate the wife by disregarding any posted pet policies and smuggle said pet(s) into motel room using techniques perfected by Pablo Escobar. Spend rest of the night in fervent prayer that every creak of the building will not trigger a fit of baying, resulting in a hefty surcharge being levied by the ethnic proprietor who smells of onions and happens to live upstairs.

And so on…

Are you freaking kidding me? Don't they realize that it can all be summed up by one question:

Do you promise to live by The Golden Rule, "do unto others as you would have them do unto you?"

Yes… you can have a dog.

No… you should be slapped and sterilized.

Having a dog is akin to marriage in that the only way it will work is if the needs and comfort of the other parties involved are always considered first. With this thought in mind, I have prepared some vows for dad:

"I, dad, take Charlie as my lawfully indentured master, to serve her every whim, from this day forward, I promise to love, honor, and obey, forsaking all others, even that finagling little goober Max. What's now yours is mine, and what's mine is mine, including, but not limited to, the motorcycle, the sleeping bag, tater tots and any personal space you may once have enjoyed, as long as we both shall live."

Uh, dad, this is the part where you say "I do"…

Charlie: On a Steel Horse I Ride

There is nothing I like better than the "G" word, "Go?". Dad tries to avoid saying it, as the immediate pandemonium it invokes is not for the faint of heart, but even him spelling it causes Max and I to lose control of our faculties.

What is this canine fascination with going mobile? Some hypothesize that it's because that dogs are always excited about going somewhere new, an idea that I totally get, as everyone knows, I'm all about the travel. But Max disagrees; he can detect the sound of dad's car arriving long before it actually comes down the street, and will be waiting at the bottom of the hill. Even though he knows that the ride will be brief, less than fifteen yards, and always arrives at the same destination, the Casa, this excites him as much as a trip to Colorado.

There's the whole "hanging my head out of the window" thing. It's the canine equivalent to speed reading, or channel surfing; LOTS of information to be assimilated, but I'm only good up to 55 MPH, then I go into information overload. much like "drinking from a fire hose". It's advantageous that Miss Ellie is usually the chariot of choice these days, as this is the speed where she is most comfortable rumbling along. Although the old Subie is fully capable of exceeding 70, she lets dad know that she's only cooperating under extreme protest.

Then there's the motorcycles. Icarus, the Honda 919, provokes little response when dad fires him up, as his voice is a bit too refined for my taste, but the yellow bike? That's a different story. Jehu is a modded out Suzuki DR650, named after the Old Testament chariot driver mentioned in the book of Kings: "and the driving is like the driving of Jehu the son of Nimshi, for he driveth furiously." Jehu's story is a bit like mine, as he and dad initially met in a pawn shop. It was dad's intent to clean up the old bike and resell him, but the crotchety old goat found his own voice and convinced dad to let him stay.

After adventures too numerous to recount, here he remains today.

All can be peaceful and quiet at the Garage de la Casa, then dad will turn the key on Jehu. All it takes is the almost imperceptible whirring of Jehu's LED headlight fan to launch me into paroxysms of joy, and I will NOT be denied until we put him through his paces. For some reason, the 55 MPH rule doesn't apply to the bike, the air must be thoroughly tasted, snuffled, ingested, and savored; first on one side, then the other, then back again ad infinitum, until dad shouts over the blast of the wind, "DANG IT, CHARLIE! PICK ONE SIDE OR THE OTHER!". I obviously ignore these instructions, as A: I'm the Charlie, and B: he will have to stop the bike to enforce discipline, and dad has the attention span of a caffeinated squirrel. By the time he finds a suitable place to pull over, something else will have seized his miniscule attention, and he will have forgotten his original intent.

So why are we dogs so fixated on "going"? My belief is that it's because, above all else, we want to be with you, and the car/truck/motorcycle affords us the best opportunity to accomplish this. Think about it; road trips offer the greatest opportunity for bonding: confined space, great tunes, truck stop jerky and plenty of time for conversation.

It just doesn't get any better; see you on the road!

Dad: Blue Monday

We have houseguests at the Casa, a tiny chihuahua named Leia and a huge walking hormone storm, a redbone hound named Wookie. More on their story later, but the point is that things are busy at the Casa and a post wasn't forthcoming today. Then dad noticed today was "Blue Monday", and between that and the political rants last night on the Golden Globe "awards", I just had to counteract all this negativity.

What is Blue Monday?

It is calculated using a series of factors in a (not particularly scientific) mathematical formula. The factors are: the weather, debt level (specifically, the difference between debt and our ability to pay), the amount of time since Christmas, and how quickly we quit going to the gym in favor of going through the drive-through at McNasty's.

It was originally conceived by a PR company but has now become an annual event.

Excuse me? Something designed to create a sense of doom created by a PR firm? Who is NOT surprised? And what was the name of this firm, Dewey, Cheatum, and Howe? Anyway, moving on...

When is Blue Monday?

The date is generally reported as falling on the third Monday in January, but can also on the second or fourth Monday, or even the Monday of the last week of January, or basically anywhere "they" need to place a holiday for a story. And too bad if it happens to fall on your birthday or anniversary.

Really? A holiday to commemorate depression? If anyone has a right to dwell on their horrible beginnings, it's a scabby dog discovered in a crate. But I've discovered that time spent dwelling on the past is time not spent flouncing in the present, or more importantly, dreaming of the future.

The two best antidotes for times of depression are A: being thankful and B: giving to others who can do nothing in return… Thanks Giving. I propose that we abolish Blue Monday in favor of an early thanksgiving, one celebrated for its true meaning and not just as a prelude to Black Friday.

And the Golden Globes that was televised last night? Should have been called the Golden Gloves. I have never seen a denser concentration of smugly self-congratulatory, hyper entitled wastes of space in my life. What is their claim to fame other than being paid massive heaps of money to pretend they're someone else? I say we celebrate instead the uncelebrated, those whose daily efforts make the world a better place.

Today, take the time to bestow your own personal Golden Globe on a previously unrecognized but deserving recipient; you will brighten someone's day, and probably won't even have to listen to a fumbling acceptance speech.

Charlie: Sunday at the Spot

The sun has only dared to challenge the fog five days out of the last forty-five, and this morning is no different. I'm in my customary spot, wadded up against dad, and the rest of the dogs look like they have been dropped from the sky, sprawled in whatever position gravity left them when they hit the bed.

Climate-wise, yesterday was much like the day dad and I met; cold, cloudy, the asphalt goose-slick greasy with dew. Most normal people would not consider this to be an auspicious day for a ride, but as it's been noted many times before, we're anything but normal. Gary had suggested some additional pics for the blog, so mom offered to follow along with Miss Ellie as we headed out to "The Spot". As you know, this area is a prime dumping ground for those dogs less fortunate, so she prepared by loading up with dog food for the inevitable encounter.

The fog was so dense that dad's visor was coated both inside and out, quickly rendering it useless, so he had to navigate through the funk without it; I did my best to assist from my customary perch with my head on his right shoulder, but I'm afraid I wasn't much help either.

As soon as we turned from the main road towards Stevie's bridge, dad spotted what he had feared; a clutch of buzzards in the ditch, gathered around a pile of plastic tarp, the last resting place of one of my kind.

This area is very difficult to police, as not only is it a large rural area in close proximity to downtown Little Rock, it is also frequented by birdwatchers, rabbit and dove hunters, and the occasional farm workers just passing through. Every harmless vehicle encountered takes on a sinister air, especially those parked on the sides of the road; dad has a habit of stopping to supposedly ask if they need assistance, but his real motive is to sneak a quick peek into their back seats.

After numerous such encounters, we made it to my spot on the road, and guess what?

It's still just a spot on the road. Even though it was once the site of a terrible time in my life, I'm now so far past that particular era that it's like I'm not even the same dog, so I guess in some ways, maybe it's not even the same spot after all.

I can only imagine that, like me, you have your personal spots, times and places of heartbreak and despair. But there comes a time to motor on down the road, and let these spots become what they were always meant to be, places to be remembered but celebrated, not vilified.

As do I; on the very spot where I once cowered in my crate, I ignored the fog and cold, and I flounced and charked and rolled and thrashed like a complete lunatic until dad finally had to use The Voice; so we saddled up and headed home to the insanity of the Casa del Whackos.

Charlie: The Final Countdown

Dad has been busy taking care of the last-minute minutiae before returning to work next week, but yesterday was an exceptionally beautiful day at the Casa, so on the bike we went.

I have many things I particularly enjoy: licking dad, laying on dad, annoying dad, sleeping with dad, bogarting dad's food, (are we seeing a pattern here?), but what I love best is riding with dad. Taking Miss Ellie is always cause for excessive celebration, but the bike?

That's what makes my heart overload.

The almost imperceptible click of the key being inserted into the ignition is all it takes to send me into quivering, paroxysmal fit of anticipation. Who gives a flying fig who's sitting in or marching on the White House when we're carving through the curves, my ears popping in the wind as it peels my floppy lips back from my choppers. This causes my teeth to dry out and my lips to stick so when we finally stop, I'm sporting a maniacal Joker-like grin.

After enough time in the saddle, I eventually calm down enough to lay my head on dad's right shoulder and go with the flow, but no matter how long the ride or how foul the conditions, I have yet to lay down in the crate to escape the cold and rain. Are you kidding me? "Cold, wet and hungry is the life for me, what I call living, some call misery" …

Riding is moving, and moving is life; there is no bad, just varying degrees of good. Even though there has been a change of plans concerning the dreamed-of blogging trips this summer, dad's new employer has been gracious enough to agree to a very generous vacation offering, so a New Mexico/Colorado trip is not out of the question.

Because that's where I'm truly in my element. No distractions, no walls, no leashes, no boundaries, no company except what we encounter on the road, no direction except forward, no leader except the front wheel. And it WILL eventually happen, as I, Charlemagne Bravissimo, have decreed it so!

The difficult we do immediately. the impossible takes a little longer…

Miss Ellie Throws a Hissy

I took dad, Charlie, and Max on a trip up the Natchez Trace Parkway last week, over five hundred miles without a hitch, but did dad mention how flawlessly I performed? Nooooooo….

On the contrary; as is so often the case when dealing with the elderly, every hint of a foul vapor is a reason to suspect another leak underneath my hood. Dad would panic at the slightest whiff, whipping over to the shoulder and perform very revealing examinations in full view of other cars whizzing by on the motorway; how would he like it if someone flipped his skirt up over his head and started poking around in his vitals?

So I've been steaming about it ever since; when mom and dad went shopping yesterday for a new car for his job, I saw my chance for revenge. Even though I know that my position at the Casa is secure, that doesn't hinder me from being a vindictive old biddy, sometimes for no other reason than just because I can.

So, they spent way too long all googly-eyed over the latest and greatest in modern technology, which gave me plenty of time to hatch a plan to remind them who was the brightest star in the automotive firmament. When on the way home, they stopped at the Taco Smell drive though, I decided to stage a hunger strike, and laid down and refused to budge. As the drive through was only one lane, dad had no choice but to get out and push, in full view of the line of honking cars behind us waiting VERY impatiently for their daily dose of flatulence inducing manna. And did I mention that this drive emptied out onto one of busiest thoroughfares in the city?

But my revenge was not yet complete.

 He has my skirt up, looking at my internals with a frowny face like he actually knows what he's doing, when a crackhead strolls by and says, "cool car! My mom used to have one just like it!"

Dad narrowed the problem down to either my battery or alternator; he was somewhat fortunate that the nearest auto parts store was only a quarter mile away, so he had no choice to pull the battery and start walking. Mom suggested that he shanghai a shopping cart from the nearby Dollar store; he refused under the belief that the only thing that could make him look any more like a homeless person would be wearing a shower cap and muttering to himself.

Mom said that there were many more similarities than just those two; dad was not pleased.

So instead, dad elected to carry the battery, first on one shoulder then the other, trudging down Main Street like a pale Kalahari bushman striding across the Serengeti with his belongings on his head, with mom trotting dutifully in his wake like some sort of transient geisha girl. After getting a charge put on the battery, the Trek of Shame was then reversed.

The official diagnosis was a failed alternator, but I have my own definition: operational interruptus aggravated by acute mechanical angst.

As retribution, Dad has me in Quiet Time at the Casa; doesn't he realize that this just gives me more time to orchestrate my next tantrum?

It's always a party at the Casa!

Charlie: Yo, Dad...

What's up, Charlie? It's 0415; you should be busy sleeping and crowding me off of the bed like usual, not waking me up with excessive face slobbers.

If you must know, it's just that I'm a bit bummed that you're going back to work tomorrow; whatever happened to you and I hoboing around the country with Miss Ellie and blogging about our experiences?

Well, Chuckilicious, that's still the dream, but sometimes dreams take a bit longer than when hatched, or even change and evolve into even bigger and better than originally conceived. It certainly doesn't mean that they're dead.

Do you still think we have something unique here?

I'm sure that everyone who has a special dog would answer that question the same way, but considering all things, the way we met, the message of the Crate, and the movement it has empowered, I would say yes, Your Charkness, it's pretty dang unique. Even though you are the very epitome of "high maintenance", your goofy presence has helped me through some especially dark times.

So, what's the plan now?

To keep spreading your message; that we all have crates in our lives, crates that others may see as intolerable but we have grown so accustomed to the confines that we refuse to be released but instead continue to embrace our bondage. But change is always an option.

But daaaaad, you were released from a particularly vile crate back in September; how do you know that tomorrow you're not just climbing into another of a different shape and color?

The short answer, Charlie? I don't, but I do believe in hope. Times and circumstances change, and paths are placed before us for us to explore; the only way to determine that a road is a dead end is to forge ahead, keeping a keen eye out for the signs. Then again, a path that appears to be dead end may simply be a detour, a temporary exit off of the freeway to refuel; it's difficult to make the necessary connections to the right people when you're flying down the interstate.

So, when's the next trip, dad?

Charlie, you know better than anyone that every time we leave the Casa, even for a short run to the hardware store, is the "next trip". But if by trip you mean another epic adventure out west, it will have to wait until summer, but never fear, it will happen; the call is too strident to ignore.

Zzzzzzzz…

Charlie!

Wha, what, dad?

How long have you been asleep, just letting me ramble on?

Uh, dad, that's what you sometimes do, whether I'm asleep or not, just figured that I would take advantage of the situation… now, if you're quite done yapping, how about a little butt scratching to escort this old girl back to the Land of Nod? There ya go, that's what I'm talking about!

'Night, Charlie; or is that "morning"?

Dad: Bull Taco

I have a good friend with Down's Syndrome who once told me "I have three boyfriends; and one of them's a Mezcan!" When I asked her how she managed to have three when many single people can't seem to to find one, she said…

"I don't know; I guess I just attrack 'em!"

Well, I guess we just attrack 'em as well. First day back at work after an extended period of un-indentured servitude; after lunch with the new boss, I'm returning to the terminal when I spot a tiny chihuahua sitting alone in the middle of the vast expanse of concrete. It seemed oddly appropriate that I had some Mexican leftovers in the car, but the little immigrant was way too savvy to allow himself to be captured while somehow still ending up with all of my enchiladas. This was especially embarrassing as he was skinny as a rail and running on three legs, as his front right one appeared to be broken.

After an extended time of ritual humiliation at the paws of the Frito Bandito, I tried a different approach, circling him a few times in the car then just nonchalantly opening the door; after a bit, he wandered over to investigate. I scooped him up, and now he thinks he's the El Presidente of the Casa.

Of no small significance to me is that it has been two years to the day that we found Charlie, so of course I had to call Zach and Tara, who just had to bring their overlord, the canine Princess Lola over to pay homage to the latest immigrant to sneak across the border.

After work, I chauffeured the micro dog over to Landmark Animal Hospital to be checked for a microchip, and also to have his leg examined. It appears that it was broken at some time in the past, but never set or casted properly; as a result, there is some atrophy of the muscles in that leg, as well as some damage to his rear legs. We went ahead and did a full checkup, no chip, no worms, no parasites, clean bill of health except for those legs. The doctor recommended against x-rays at this time, as fixing this problem would involve a specialist who would no doubt want to do their own exam anyway.

According to the vet, chihuahuas are frequently deserted in that part of town, particularly when they have some sort of defect, so here we are. The name Don Fredo doesn't seem to fit him, so mom started calling him Bull Taco in homage to the famous Spanish motorcycle manufacturer Bultaco.

He likes to be called Bull.

He also apparently likes mom better, the little traitor.

He is obviously going to require some special care, as he can't jump up on the beds of the Casa. For this reason, I was considering adopting him out to a more suitable domicile, but I'm pretty sure that this action would now result in mom forcibly removing some of my more personal body parts.

So, does he complete his immigration process and become a legal citizen of the Casa? Or does he decide to buck the system and continue to evade the border patrol? You'll have to ask him, as I'm sure that he will have much to say on the subject. As for me, I'm starting to feel like Josey Wales; after setting off on his journey alone, he somehow managed to acquire an entourage, prompting the following:

"I suppose that mangy red-bone hound's got no place else to go either…

He might as well ride along with us; Hell, everybody else is!"

Max: Senor Bultaco el Vivaracho de la Casa del Whackos

Max here: between Bull's limited command of the English language and the difficulty he has typing and using Google Translate due to his injured right wing, I will be helping him post until he can attend some night classes at the local community college.

From what I can piece together from his story, his original name was simply Hector, and he was born on Cinco de Mayo in Guadalajara, Mexico in the year of our Lord 2014. His earliest memories are of helping to cultivate the family farm, his job being to manicure and package the sticky green buds before they were shipped north to Colorado. When his family learned of the upcoming federal building project that may be soon forthcoming at the border, they decided to send young Hector north to find his fortune.

Crossing scorpion laden deserts(both the two- and eight-legged variety) and swimming the muddy Rio Grande (well, wading for most, but he's a little guy), he suffered many treacherous miles; it was on such a night that the desert moon illuminated his first encounter with a band of bloodthirsty banditos; although he left them laying motionless in the very spot where they thought to leave him, the experience left him with the crippled right arm that afflicts him to this day. His daring actions to defend other himself and other refugees earned him the title of El Zurdo, "the Lefty", leaving envious males and grateful females in his wake all up and down the border. Eventually his exploits attracted him some unwanted attention from the Chihuahua Cartel, and he had to slip across the border at Boquillas into the relative safety of the Land of the Yanquis.

At this time, he wasn't traveling alone; more on his traveling companion in a later post…

In an effort to build a new life, he decided to change his name to something a bit more memorable than Hector, but not as sinister as El Zurdo. It was during this time that he was holed up in a barn with another undocumented immigrant, Manuel Labor, when they found a dust covered Bultaco motorcycle stashed back in the shadows. After much tinkering and cursing under his breath(his mamacita would have washed his mouth out with sopa had she heard him), he and Manuel coaxed the old machine back to life. Hector became so aggressive on the bike, charging across the dry Chihuahuan desert, pinning the throttle with his crippled right paw that Manuel began calling him el Toro, the Bull.

Bultaco seemed a little less threatening, and the name stuck.

Bull wandered here and there, sometimes trotting, sometimes hitching rides with friendly truck drivers and vacationing families. He was working his way across the southwest when he received word that there was a benevolent dictator at a place called the Casa del Whackos in Arkansas, where he could find a decent health care plan and recover from his previous injuries.

Through a stroke of luck(or was it divine providence?), the last ride he hitched left him at the trucking terminal where dad had started working that very day.

So here he sits, acting like he's been here his entire life instead of just one week.

Viva la Bultaco!

Dad: Weekend Update

It's a unseasonably warm February morning, which brings up memories of posting from the back porch of the Casa. A parade of dogs trots through my mind, not the least being Stevie, who loved nothing better that hanging out at my feet, lazily watching the hummingbirds through that janky eye, so I thought I would do a quick update on the current inmates.

Angel: Angel is an old girl, and the matriarch of the Casa; she loves to patrol the perimeter, sometimes barking at nothing, but she almost paid for this behavior with her life. Mom let her back in the other night from her nightly rounds only to find Angel bleeding profusely from her left shoulder, apparently a result of an encounter with the pack of feral dogs down the street. 300.00 later and enough stitches to make Frankenstein envious, she is now bumping around the Casa sporting the Cone of Shame. On a positive note, we can now receive programming on the TV never before possible with tin foil on the rabbit ears.

Echo: St Echo of Cardiogram spends the majority of her time at the Casa del Alex, but when she does come home, delights on bounding madly around the palatial estate in a failed attempt to find her own dignity.

Bull Taco: Bull's gimp is showing improvement, but he still plays the sympathy card for all it's worth. He has developed a raspy cough that always seems to manifest itself when mom starts to put him outside, which I personally think is no coincidence. On the other paw, the micro dog is fearless; when the feral dogs wandered too close to the Casa during daytime hours, he charged them like a three-legged Don Quixote. The bullies tucked tail and fled, probably in shock at the prospect of being devoured by a tiny tan velociraptor.

Max: The Patron Saint for the Perpetually Worried is still engaging in daily warfare with Mia the Imp, recently featured in her high school yearbook as "Most Annoying with Absolutely No Respect for Personal Space".

And Charlie? Well, after two years, The Charles reached a new milestone last night. She was engaging in her nightly obsession with compulsive face licking when mom dared me to play a little game of Russian Roulette by attempting to open and close my mouth before Charlie could take advantage of my stupidity. The first attempt was a resounding success for me, and I should have stopped the game there, but as has been noted before, I'm not the sharpest tool in the shed.

Have you ever seen those slow-motion videos of a frog's tongue flicking out three times the length of its own body to make a meal of an unsuspecting bug?

Well, after what I experienced, I consider the bug lucky. Before I could realize the depths of my own stupidity, Charlie had finished an extensive dental and tonsil examination, and was looking to extend her expertise into the fields of gastrointestinal and upper respiratory infection. Only my extensive training in the manly martial art of Tae Kwon Koughing and Sputtering saved me from total defilement.

And the hummingbirds? They're laying low for the time being, but I am preparing for an all-out assault of the voracious little ingrates this spring.

When dealing with the feathered Mongolian hordes, peace through superior firepower is my new strategy.

Max: The Casa del Whackos Workout Plan

Max here; since dad has went back to work, he has packed on a few pounds. In a humanitarian effort to prevent him from looking any more than he already does like a fire plug with thinning hair, the inmates at the Casa have devised a daily workout plan.

0300: advanced hot yoga session involving the Inverted Dog and pre-Sunrise Salutation positions to lever out of bed when nature calls, or Mia decides that she's hasn't annoyed anyone recently enough… 250 calories

0305: Multiple laps to and from the back door to let inmates in and out, and in and out, then in, then out, etc, according to their respective biorhythms… 300 calories

0315: Jumping to Conclusions, followed by toe contractions, 10 reps; this exercise involves dad's bare foot coming into contact with what he assumes is the product of Bultaco's overactive urinary tract, only to discover that

Charlie has once again managed to get more water on the floor than down her gullet... 575 calories.

0325: deadlift. This is where either Charlie or Bultaco have decided to exercise squatter's rights to the warm spot on the bed that dad has vacated during his rigorous workout and must be forcibly moved. All of the dogs are capable of giving Oscar-worthy performances when feigning sleep, in an effort to move dad to the couch, where they will eventually set up camp as well... 125-5000 calories, according to which dog requires eviction.

We then give him a short interval to recover until the opportunity clock erupts and it's time to WATCH HIM GET DRESSED! Will it be blue jeans or khakis? Dress pants or riding gear? We watch these clothing choices with rapt anticipation, as this determines to what extent we will be participating in the days activities. I realize that this part of the regimen doesn't seem like much of a workout for dad, and you are correct, usually only good maybe 100 calories... that is, until you take the dog-factor into consideration.

What should be only four steps from the bed to the closet becomes an almost impassable Canine Gauntlet trying to predict which way dad is going next; when he swerves to keep from stepping on the Bull, Charlie is there to divert him towards me, who in turn steers him towards Mia that she may cover his pants with hair. The fact that it's great fun to witness dad's half-clad portly pirouettes is just an added benefit to the morning's sessions. By the time he finishes his workout with multiple laps to get coffee, then to the car, then back inside as he forgot his keys, then twenty reps with the lint brush as the morning light has exposed the fact that his pants legs are reminiscent of Esau's, dad will easily have burned though at least 5000 calories. At this rate, we'll have him in supermodel shape long before bikini season arrives…

…except for one thing; there is a Daylight Donuts directly between the Casa and the terminal, and those cinnamon twists and kolaches aren't just going to "eat themselves", are they?

We always have a big time at the Casa del Whackos!

Bull Taco: Le Bull de la Taco

Psst… que pasa, Charlee?

What's up, Bultaco?

How does one know when one ees truly an inmate of zee Casa, and not intransiente'?

Well, Bull, there is no vetting process, you just show up and kind of stick around, and you eventually become family. The same is true of my siblings around the world; most show up in the beginning just to check out the train wreck that is the Casa del Whackos and quickly transform from casual observers to inmates.

But how does one know REALLY know that a change of address ees not in my future? That I weel not be deported?

Well, one sign is when you stake out your claim on the bed; another is when you start getting invited along for rides to the hardware store, trips to Sonic, or even aimless drives "just because". But in my case, as well of that of Miss Ellie, Stevie, et al, I knew I was a permanent fixture when I found my voice; it's a lot more difficult for dad to re-home a dog that has the ability to divulge what REALLY goes on behind the scenes of the Casa, at least until the statute of limitations expires.

Zees ees great news! I must send immediate word to mi familia in the old country, that they might begeen their journey's north!

You might want to re-think that decision, Bull; between Max, Mia, Angel, and myself, the dad-lovin's are getting spread pretty thin as it is. Do you really want to bring more dogs into the equation?

Oh, Charlee, you must learn to theenk outside zee box; I have zee secret weapon!

Oh? What's that?

Mi nuevo mamacita! I weel make her MY loyal subject! While you and Papa are on trips on le motorcyclia, I weel cast mi spell on her! I weel hog her side of zee bed! Her burritos shall be MI burritos!

Yo, Bull…

Si, Charlee?

You're not as helpless as you look.

Charlie: Time in a Throttle

Some people say that dogs have no sense of time, based on the fact that we're just as ecstatic to see you after five minutes as after five days. The sound of dad's car pulling up in the driveway triggers a paroxysm of joy that can only eventually be subdued by bolting madly around the yard, then into the Casa carrying at least half of the yard with me on my great white hooves.

At least that's mom's approximation; dad's told her a million times to stop exaggerating.

When dad hits the ignition on the motorcycle, the seconds that pass before we can get moving stretch into an eternity of anticipation; but our time spent together on the bike seems to pass in a microsecond.

It hardly seems fair, does it?

People wonder why dad and I ride together; is it the attention factor of taking a dog on a motorcycle? To spread the message of the Crate? Just because it's "fun"? As far as I'm concerned, any reason at all is fine by me, but the real reason is much simpler.

Time.

The average lifespan of a dog is between 10-15 years compared to threescore and ten of a human; this brief period of time where our paths intersect vanishes all to quickly, never to return. It's imperative that we milk every iota from every second we have together in this life, as it's obvious we have been granted a rare gift, an opportunity to combine two of the finest experiences; dogs and motorcycles.

It just doesn't get any better.

When we ride, invariably someone will always comment on how dangerous it must be, is she strapped in? don't you worry? etc… of course dad worries; he's a human. He's always reaching back to see if I'm still there, choosing the route with the least traffic, and performing countless calculations to ensure we arrive aimlessly at our destination we didn't have planned, wherever that may or may not be.

However, I refuse to worry, as I have faith in dad, just as you should have faith in your personal Father, however you envision Him to be. Life is an awesome ride that sometimes involves accidents, speeding tickets (dad calls them "performance awards"), traffic jams and foul weather; the harder you twist the throttle, the faster everything, good and not so good, seems to come rushing at you.

While the "bad" experiences tend to stand out in our minds, the actual reality is that the vast majority of the journey involves none of these things. The hum of the tires, the throb of the engine, the constant approach of the ever-elusive horizon are the real text of the story, the bad experiences are simply the punctuation; without them, the story would just run together.

Much like one of dad's eternal sentences.

Besides, statistics show that many more people die in hospital beds every day than in motorcycle accidents in a year…

I think it's high time that we do something about those dastardly beds!

Dad: A new Inmate at the Casa?

It sounds like there is a new inmate at the Casa del Whackos; wait, wait, before everyone gets their knickers in a twist, let me explain.

Yesterday morning, Charlie was doing what Charlie does best, which is whatever Charlie wants to do at the particular instant. This time she was sprawled out on the bed, demanding that I, her indentured servant, scratch her brisket. She must have been a tad more relaxed than usual, as the most unusual sound began emanating from somewhere in the vicinity of the south end of a northbound Charlie.

It startled her as much as it did me, both of us looking at the other in stunned disbelief; what could possibly be making such as prolonged, high pitched, squeaking noise? Was it dangerous? Why would it not show itself? After a brief period of tension-filled silence, there it was again:

SQUREEEEEEEAAAAAWWWWKKK!!!

And that's when it dawned on us; it was the clarion call of the elusive Barking Crack Spider; after a bit of research, we discovered that this particular species makes its home beneath the tails of certain dogs that consume inordinate volumes of canned Alpo. While usually not life threatening, their sour demeanor makes them a challenging choice as service animals, although their "attributes" often go unnoticed when visiting nursing homes.

So now all we have to do is catch it and convince mom to let us keep it. In the meantime, she has already began raising some unwelcome questions: who will feed and clean up after it? How will we ever find a collar and leash that will fit? When and how do we spay or neuter, so we don't have a whole nursery full of baby crack spiders filling the night with their tiny barks?

I am convinced we will eventually capture and tame the wee noisome varmint, and the little guy will fit right right in with the rest of the misfits of the Casa del Whackos.

As you know, a "Chark" is a Charlie bark… we shall dub this one "Chart".

Charlie: All the news that's (not) fit to print

Did you hear about the passenger that was forcibly removed from the United flight? Or that Madonna attempted to adopt another child? Or that Bruce Jenner…. I give up; I don't even want to go there.

At the Casa, we dropped cable long ago, and while that is not an euphemism for what I do in the back yard, the results are the same. Dad has been traveling on business a little more than usual, and the first response when checking into a motel is to do what? Toss your bags on the bed and grab the remote, allowing the sewage to flow the wrong way. Channel after channel of strife and confusion, is it any wonder that sleep comes at such difficulty? Hours after the time that Bull Taco and I would have demanded that he and mom turn out the lights, dad is still mindlessly clicking through the channels like a junkie scrambling for a fix.

Upon hearing him describe this situation upon his return, it occurred to me that the media is nothing more than just another form of my crate. How so, you ask? In my case, my crate was a vile situation from which there was no apparent alternative; even after being released from my crate, my first impulse was to voluntarily return. It wasn't until I was made to realize that there is a better way, a permanent escape, if you will.

I once heard the theory that we are hard wired as a species to only hear as much bad news as we could personally affect; first our families, then our tribes, then maybe our cities, but never much more than that. Now we are bombarded daily with words of crisis from around the globe, situations over which we have absolutely no control, so overwhelmed by the onslaught that we tend to shut down emotionally; if we can't fix it all, why fix anything? But I'm here to tell you...

You can.

One of the benefits of backcountry travel is the enforced separation from the constant fluorescent hum of media buzz. Once we camped by a lake in New Mexico, so clear and smooth that it was impossible to tell where the actual Milky Way ended and its reflection in the lake's surface started. Even though the temperature began to plummet in the wee hours, it was such an amazing sight that we were unwilling to mar the moment with even as much as a campfire.

This is why we travel, not so much to separate ourselves from that which is not important, but more so to reconnect to that which "is". Dad always says, "life begins after the second tank of gas" and I guess that could be true, as long as you're heading in the right direction, and not just buzzing around in confused circles like some sort of mechanized June bug.

So here we go again; the travel bug has bit hard and infected us with a virulent case of wanderlust. Preparations have begun for another walkabout next month; where will we go? It doesn't really matter, as long as it's dusty and remote, where the oxygen may be thin but the sense of connection is not. Where the shackles of media connection are nonexistent, and the only news that can reach us is what we conjure up ourselves in that very moment.

Pack your saddlebags and climb on; you're going with us.

Charlie: Priorities

There's an old saying "I would rather sleep with a wet dog than a guilty conscience"; last night, dad got both. Mom decided that Max and I needed a spa day, so dad dutifully trudged to the shower to fulfill his destiny as beautician/masseuse/cosmetician. The time it takes a dog to dry is directly proportional to the lateness of the hour, so, last night, the bed retained a slightly swamp-like atmosphere.

Mom wisely relocated to the west wing of the Casa del Whackos.

Some mentioned on this blog that dad and I must be getting "royalties" whenever another site picks up my story, then litters it with ads; dad responded somewhat peevishly with "not a dime!". They quickly set him straight with the reminder that this story is not about profit, it's all about the story about the crates that we all inhabit at one time or another.

And they are right.

Although we appreciate it when someone else puts my story out there, we find it a bit off putting when they chop it up with questionable advertising in an attempt to make a shekel or three. Dad and Gary have considered this many times, but in the end, always err on the side of caution and leave the banners and misdirects to the other guys.

It reminds me of the passage when Jesus said of the Pharisees, "verily, they have their reward". What would I choose, to profit financially from the story by telling it once, or to profit spiritually from the story by living it daily?

That's a no-brainer to this old girl.

Take today for instance: rainy Monday in Arkansas, most are stressing about the start of another work week, but not me! Mom is making coffee, Max and Mia are cavorting at the foot of the bed, Bultaco has yet to emerge from the Cavern of the Covers, and me? I'm where I should be, sprawled out on dad, obtusely oblivious to the fact that he too must eventually rise and shine.

It's great to be the Queen!

Bull Taco: somewhere along zee border

A full moon casts a long shadow, that of a lone figure with an impressive set of ears, as he stealthily makes his way towards the mighty Rio Grande. His nombre is El Zurdo, The Lefty, a moniker not taken but earned in a cantina brawl along the dry Chihuahua desert; the other participants in the fracas earned no such names in the encounter.

They're all dead.

El Zurdo is on a mission to transport the fruit of of his family's farm, his destination is the dispensaries located far north in the mythical land of Colorado. That such a diminutive figure can not only carry but conceal such an aromatic load is a testament to both the brawn and brains of the sinewy canine.

His contact had apprised him of a secret tunnel that would travel under the Wall being constructed along the border, but even this approach carried its own set of dangers. This gateway was owned and maintained by a rival family who contracted their security services to the dreadful Los Gatos, a shadowy cadre of depraved reprobates so evil that even the Kardashian Klan gave them wide berth.

The entrance to the tunnel was concealed deep in the midst of the Gatos stronghold, the Litterbox del Muerto: Zurdo picked his way through the sandy minefield, the ammonia-like stench causing his hackles to bristle and the bile to rise in his throat. The darkness of the passageway drew him inexorably onward, and with one last longing thought of a special senorita back in Juarez, he plunged into its inky depths.

The tunnel began to constrict as it vanished into the rocky depths, and it occurred to El Zurdo that every foot that he descended equated to many more metric tons of unstable rock suspended above his head. The clarion bells of claustrophobia had begun to clatter in his cranium when he sensed a new danger in the darkness ahead, an unseen presence so reprehensible that it could only be worthy of one fate:

Violent death at the paws of Los Crippled One!

He stealthily approached the unseen foe, coiling himself into the killing machine whose name struck icy fear into the hearts of those who would do evil and adoration in those that would do good, and then he pounced. His razor-like incisors lanced through the torpid flesh of his mortal foe, and a horrible shriek filled the fetid air of the darkness…

Uh, Bull? That's the covers you're under, not some sort of cave; and if you don't mind, could you ease up a bit on my hand? I've grown accustomed to having two of them…

Uh, lo siento, mi padre.

Go back to sleep, Bull…

Buenos nachos, papi.

Dad: Vaya con Dios, Max E. Million…

I don't have it in me to be witty or creative right now, so I'll cut to the chase:

Max is gone.

Earlier tonight, I thought it odd that he wasn't glued to my side as he usually is, so I began checking the cars to make sure he hadn't stowed away; no luck. After checking the house, I looked out the back door and saw a pile of brown fur out in the backyard; it was Max, alive, but just barely. I won't go into detail, but it was as bad as I've ever seen. Mom had seen the neighbor's farm dogs, two Pyrenees and a collie, in the yard earlier, and we're 99% sure that they're responsible.

The owner lives down a gated road, and either ignored me beating the crap out of his gate or wasn't home. We called the sheriff who came out to file a report and inspect the body, but what could he really do? I had no choice but to bury Max under by the light of the full moon.

Max was my dog, my only dog, for a long time until Charlie came along. I would be doing him a massive injustice to even attempt to eulogies him, as no words can do him justice.

There are two holes involved here, one in the backyard, and one in my heart;

RIP, Max; you surely deserved better.

And then...

Dad here; I apologize for the lack of response for your overwhelming offering of condolences, but it's been a somewhat of a blur. Since the beginning of Charlie's story, I have made it a point to read and acknowledge every comment with at least a "like", as I figure that's the very least I can do to acknowledge the fact that each of you took time to comment. The problem I'm having now is that A; there are so many, and B: they are so heartfelt and well written than I can only get through a couple at a time before my pucker reflex activates, but I promise you that I will get through them all.

I've had many dogs, but Max was part of a cadre who's loyalty defied description; Uki, Beebe, Max, and Charlie. He had the distinction of coming along at a time when there were no others to with which to share the attention, then had the misfortune to be here when his sun was partially eclipsed by the elemental force of nature that is Charlie.

Max and I were inseparable through three surgeries, innumerable road trips, good times, very bad times. He loved to hang out with the boys when Zach and I would be tinkering with the bikes in the garage, always worrying that we were going to somehow sneak off without him.

And worrying? He carried a Ph D in fretting, the only real time that he would truly relax is when we were in the car together, as he knew there was no escaping him.

When I would have to leave on motorcycle and/or business trips, he transferred this huge mass of loyalty to

Mom and Alex, and everyone that visited the Casa was instantly adopted by Max as not a visitor but a sibling.

To be honest, I've always felt a twinge of guilt that Max's thunder was partially diminished by Charlie's lightning, and now that the hairy little goober has passed, that twinge has grown into a stabbing pain. Think of Woody and Buzz from "The Toy Story", and you'll get a snapshot of the situation. Now the emptiness in my heart is only matched by the emptiness behind my knees, as the last thing I would see every night is Max's hairy fanny disappearing under the covers en route to his favorite sleeping spot.

Over the last two days, I've wondered if Bull Taco entered the scene to ease the sting of Max's imminent departure, but if that was the cure, it sure isn't working. Bull is a special dog, and no doubt will continue to grow into his own particular role, but there will never be another Max E Million. Just remembering him now makes it feel like a flare up of diverticulitis, as the pain in my gut is actually physical.

But life goes on, and this too shall pass. Charlie has been remarkably subdued, but I know with a certainty that will change. Mia has been acting a bit perplexed as well, as Max was the target of her particular brand of devilry every morning, and Bull? As long as he has a lap, front seat or motorcycle tank bag to occupy, Bull is chill with almost any situation.

So now the Casa crew is down to four; most normal people would think that this is more than enough, but in case you haven't noticed, we're anything but normal.

This is freaking miserable: miss you terribly, Max.

Ode to the Max

I remember the day I first met you
In the mountains full of rain and thick fog
You stayed still and so quiet, until we reached home that night
Then instantly became a new dog.

You were there before all the others
Through difficult times full of strife
Many miles east and west, perched on the armrest
Traveling together down the highway of life

Your presence is still constant as always
The memories will always be warm
What easily could be viewed by some as just needy
Was devotion in its true form

Your lesson will long be remembered
Spring, summer, winter and fall
It is better to have loved, to loved hard and lost
Than to never have loved at all.

(Although between me and you, I sometimes don't really believe it)

We'll meet again, ya hairy little goober…

Charlie: Forgiveness Sets You Free

Since my metamorphosis from the crate two years ago, much has been said about my previous "owners"; do I resent them? Do I wonder if they are aware of how far I have progressed?

The gospel truth is, I don't give it a moment's consideration.

I say this not out of bitterness, but based on the fact that he who angers you controls you, and I am the Charles; if even dad can't control me, why would I let someone else have the honor?

At threescore and ten, a human's life is short enough as it is, and a dog's life is shorter still, much too short to be spent confined by the shackles of another's making. I instead choose to live in a state of what dad calls "joyful abandon", every mile I travel is with the throttle wide open.

Granted, this sometimes doesn't translate well into "polite" society, but I am Charlemagne Bravissimo, and I careth not. I spend absolutely no time concerning myself with such mundane facts. I let dad deal with the consequences of my charking, flouncing, thrashing, splashing, the sound of his exasperated voice fading in the distance is like a beautiful symphony to this girl's ears.

Consider the tragic passing of Max; it would be very easy to carry bitterness and malice towards the dogs that did the actual damage, or the owner who shows absolutely no remorse, but what does that gain? It won't bring the hairy little goober back to life, but I don't believe for a minute that even if it did, Max himself would carry malice in his heart; it's not in a dog's nature to dwell on the past.

There's a reason why the view over the handlebars is many times larger than that of the reflection in the rear view mirrors; although you do need to consider from whence you came, don't you think the future is much more exciting?

Charlie: Happy Easter from the Casa del Whackos!

Dad was raised in church but has always cautioned me to keep religion out of my posts. A: there are other places for that, and B: more times than not, the "religious" approach is either so heavy handed that it unnecessarily offends or so saccharine that it sickens.

On our last trip out west, dad met a self-proclaimed agnostic follower of my scribblings in Moab, UT who said," I have to ask; are you a Christian?". He didn't know it, but he had given dad a huge compliment, because that statement told us that the posts had made him pause and consider without being offended.

It would be very easy to draw the analogy between the story of the crate and the story of the tomb, but even I won't go there. As tempting as it is to compare the relationship between man and God to that between dad and myself, that love provides much better motivation than the threat of eternal punishment, such a comparison skirts a little too close to sacrilege.

I'm a simple-minded dog, and I respond to a simple-minded message, so regardless of who you call "dad" on this Easter Sunday, please consider:

Without Him, there would be no "this".

Charlie: E-Motion

There are three types of people on this planet: people who don't like dogs, people who like the "idea" of dogs, then there are dog people. The second category seems to be the largest, but fortunately the mindless fanaticism of those of us in the third more than compensates for the other two.

We dogs are simply descendants of wolves, and as such, we thrive on the interaction with the rest of the pack. The worst form of abuse for a dog is not necessarily infliction of pain, but simply that of neglect and boredom. It blows my mind to see someone bring home a cute puppy, only to later put him/her out on a chain to be forgotten; one of these days, dad will probably find himself behind bars after a confrontation with one of these heartless cretins.

Anyone who thinks that dogs don't experience emotion obviously doesn't have enough sense to remember how to put the toilet paper on the roll (over the top, of course). Just a few examples of those experienced at the Casa del Whackos:

Jealousy? Just let dad mention another dog's name, let alone even act like he's going to give some dog lovin's, and the green-eyed monster immediately joins the already crowded cast at the Casa.

Guilt? You won't see much of that around here, as we all know we can do no wrong, regardless of the devastation we visit upon the interior of the Subaru. Although Pride can be used to describe the feeling of accomplishment after Bull Taco leaves an impressive pile of Tootsie Rolls for dad to find with his bare feet.

Curiosity? Desire? Lust? Avarice? Greed? Gluttony? If you want to see all these emotions exhibited simultaneously, just open up the fridge, or rattle some plastic in the kitchen.

Joy? This is easy; just let dad even ACT like he is going roll the motorcycle out of the garage. It doesn't matter how engrossed I am in my flouncing in the ditch; I can hear the "click" of the ignition and the whine of the starter from a mile away, and I come charging. Between the yowling, charking, and the mad rush to leap up on the bike, dad has resigned himself that the start of every ride will result in eardrum and/or soft tissue damage.

But Trust is the emotion that we convey the best. No matter what life throws at us, it can be immediately forgotten with just a touch of the master's hand, and all the negative emotions are replaced with happy, relaxed, calm, peaceful emotions; at least until Mia makes a move on the rawhide, or Bull Taco decides he wants to reclaim his spot on dad, then peace goes out the window, and it's time to get it on…

Ya'll come see us this summer if you ever find yourself in Arkansas; Bashful is not an emotion we have a problem with!

Dad: RIP, Senor Bull Taco

Dad here; Bull Taco's time at the Casa del Whackos was cut short in a particularly violent manner, and I'm not a bit interested in sharing the gory intricacies of yesterday's tragedy. Two scriptures in the Bible sometimes seem to not square with each other: Ecclesiastes 9:11 "chance happeneth to all dogs" and Romans 8:28, "all things work together for the good".

As dad, I want to "fix" things, but I have to realize that some things will never be fixable, or that the fixing exceeds my skill level, not always an easy thing to admit, but here we are,

Wherever "here" is.

But I don't want to stay here, gotta keep moving on; Bull is gone, but the mission is not.

I can't begin to explain the level of tragedy that has befallen the Casa del Whackos since this page started, so I won't even try. Just like Max and Stevie Mae, Bull Taco's time was short and his stature was tiny, but his impact was massive. Let it be known that the joy brought by these little goobers far outweighed the anguish incurred at their passing.

The basis of this page has never been to avoid bad news, but to instead use the bad to focus on the good that can come out of any situation, so I'll leave you with this:

Yesterday was Take Your Child To Work Day, so I did, and this time it was the Bull. It was a beautiful spring day and I had no worries about Bull being affected by the heat, so hippity-hop up into the car he went. On the way back home, he demanded a stop at the Taco Bell drive through, and that's how I will remember him: perched in a sea of crumbs in the passenger seat, demanding that I bequeath upon him the vast majority of my Crunchy Beef Burrito, and that's where he will ride forever, at least in my heart and memory.

I can barely see the road.

Dad: Skinny Minnie

A few years ago, a "friend" used to spend his lunch hour fishing at a secluded spot by the Arkansas River. He came back telling me of a friendly black dog who had apparently been abandoned and wanted me to go pick it up and keep it "just for the weekend"; yeah, right. I did take her some food, but we didn't have room at the Casa; the "Unreasonable Bug" had not yet bit.

Or so I thought.

What I didn't put together until just today was that this girl had been dumped in the same general area where we found Charlie, Stevie, Beau, et al, some years later.

Anyway, mom, Alex and I went to see a movie that night. As we walked out, a huge line of thunderstorms was approaching from the west, and all I could think about was that goofy black dog down by the river. And this is NOT the place you want to be heading on a Friday night, the actual name of the boat ramp was Outlaw Landing, named by the locals due to the nefarious activities that always seem to be occurring there. The area was so bad that the police actually shut it down, and the road was eventually bulldozed.

But there we went, bag of dog food on hip, can of Deep Woods Off and pistol in pocket. As our headlights illuminated the desolate scene, the clouds of mosquitoes parted to reveal the black girl curled up in a hole, motionless except for what would become her trademark:

Her thumping tail.

We loaded her up into the back of the car, and she turned out to be the happiest dog that has ever resided at the Casa; even when she was in deep doo doo with mom for eating the chickens, her tail could not stop wagging. Although it was years ago that she spent a short time as an inmate, she is still regarded as one of the most remarkable dogs that ever graced the Casa del Whackos.

I'm sure you're thinking "but what does this have to do with Bull Taco?" Well, since you asked, I'll tell you…

There are some dogs that have made their mark over the passage of years, dogs like Uki the Wonder Dog, Beebe King, Max E. Million. And then there are a select few like Stevie Mae and Skinny that are so special that, like a shooting star, they make an indelible impression in a very short time.

Bull was one of these, x10.

I didn't even think that I particularly liked Chihuahuas until the slick-headed little bandito made the Casa his lair, now I can't quit thinking about getting another. Too soon? Maybe, maybe not; as you know, things have a strange way of working out around here.

And as to the dogs that brought about Max and Bull's demise, trust me when I tell you that the situation is being taken care of in the proper manner. I'm sure that some would like to hear all the details, but I promise you, you do not. All I will tell you is that Thursday afternoon, I discovered that this old fat man can still cover some real estate; I was barefoot when I first heard Bull's screams, and while I don't remember touching the ground, the bottoms of my feet bear testimony that I evidently did.

We be of one blood, ye and I.

Charles: Dream On

Sunday morning at the Casa; line after line of storms have marched through the area, and if the past is any indication of the future, there will be more forthcoming. That's the thing about storms; as long as we're alive, we can count on them occurring. If the approaching fronts happen to be far enough apart to give us time to recover, storms are sometimes nothing more than a inconvenience, or even a pleasant diversion.

But it's when they come back to back in quick succession that they can test our resolve. Trees fall when their support systems are weakened by constant rainfall, then the wind and hail complete the tragedy trifecta, the trees fall and your nerves are then further tested by the incessant cacophony of chainsaws.

So here we are. The twin storms of Max and Bull Taco has weakened the root system a bit, causing dad to question some of our past and even future behavior. What if something were to happen to me out in the mountains? What if he had to tell this same story about another dog? Instead of bold and daring, what if our actions were suddenly seen as stupid and reckless? What if? What if? What if???

Well, what the freaking if?

I didn't survive my incarceration in the crate to trade its claustrophobic confines for another prison cell constructed of my own fear, or anyone else's, for that matter. Max and

Bull lived to go on trips with Miss Elsie, but the bike is MY lifeline.

Bull was an indomitable little warrior. Although the outcome was tragic, I can't help but think that this exactly how he would have wanted his story to end, a miniature Don Quixote charging full tilt at an overwhelming enemy, dad bringing up the rear like a pudgy Sancho Panza that had misplaced his mule.

Sometimes the dream doesn't end up the way we see it playing out in our minds, but that doesn't mean that we don't keep chasing that dream. And living my story IS a dream; not in some ethereal sweet by and by, but in a sometimes nasty now and now. And come what may, we're going to keep living the dream.

I know dogs, and that's exactly how Stevie, Max, and Bull Taco would have wanted it, and even if they didn't, that's how it would be. For I am Charlemagne Bravissimo, Lady Charles the Nubian Princess, the Warrior of the Wasteland, the Czarina of Chark, the Ayatollah of Rock and Rolla.

as it is written, so shall it be done.

Charlie: Unleash the Kraken

 I don't think that dad gets that the purpose of an exorcism is to cast the demon out, not invite him in, but here we are.

He made the mistake of going by the Pulaski County Humane Society last night, you know, just to check things out. There was a quartet of rowdy pups that used their superior intellects to bamboozle dad; one in particular must have had formal acting training as he appeared somewhat more sedate than the other three.

I'm believe I'm beginning to see the formation of a conspiracy; remember Rusty's Treats, the sweet potato dog treats that Max and Bull were so fond of? Well, Ms Jody had sent a memorial that just happened to be burning a hole in dad's pocket, an amount that exactly covered the little thespian's adoption fee, so what was he supposed to do? Willpower has never been one of dad's strong characteristics.

On the way home, peace and quiet was the rule of the day, with the tiny canine wedged behind dad's head as he drove to the Casa. What a sweet little dog, right? WRONG! As soon as they got home, an immediate transformation occurred; dad didn't just open the car door...

He unleashed the kraken.

Confucius says, "when another woman enters the front door, peace flies out the back"; this is also true of scruffy little wads of rampaging puppy flesh; does this dog EVER just chill out? The closest we have come to a name so far is

Taz, as in Tasmanian Devil; another option is Pilot, as he tends to pilot here and pilot there around the faux hardwood floors of the Casa.

All I know is the I, Charlemagne Bravissimo, hereby decree that the bed is a place to sleep, not a porta potty; the little spaz has only been here one night and has already anointed the bedsheets twice. His razor-sharp teeth and toenails, coupled with his willingness to use them, have already been employed in the destruction of dad's wardrobe at the Battle of Dockers Hill, and future skirmishes are no doubt on the horizon.

Mom always had a thing for the bad boys and thinks this one is a cutie as well, but he's not fooling us; dad and I see right through to the evil that resides in this imp's devilish little heart.

It's going to take a bit more than a few sprinkles of Holy Water to calm this beast!

Dad: Feliz dia de la madre?

; 0645 at the Casa. I'm trying my best to let mom sleep in, but there is a revolving parade of needy inmates demanding attention.

Mia the Unsullied, who, much to her chagrin, has escaped her last incarceration unhumped, is the first to lead the charge. I'm pretty sure that there was an anteater somewhere back in her family tree, as she can snake a tongue far enough into an ear canal to make Qtips obsolete. This process must be exacerbated be pinning one to the mattress with her foreclaws, until...

...here comes the lumbering wildebeest; one swipe of her mighty horns clears a path to the watering hole. She plops herself down in the mire and begins lathering my face with her tongue; wait a minute, that's not just any Serengeti bovine, that's the Charles! Hey, Charlie, what's up? Not much, dad, just finished washing my loins, thought I would jump up here and share the wealth; is mom up yet?

Darting their way in and out of this miasma of animals is a pack of giggling hyenas, actually only one, but that one so active that it seems like a hundred. That would be The Pup Previously Known as Yolo el Guapo, who mom has renamed Bolo, then Ajax, on his ever-present quest to prove that he is the most annoying dog to ever prance into the Casa.

This revolving cadre of inmates demanding attention continues until the carousel is brought to a screeching halt by the sound of Angel the Perpetually Mouthy Who Is On Her Own Personal Time Schedule demanding to be let back in. On her return from the back door, mom uses her bare foot to find a land mine apparently deposited by a passing bull elephant, but actually a Mother's Day gift from Ajax.

Her response was a Freudian slip of epic proportions: she meant to call him "Snicklefritz" but instead blurted out "Pickle Schitz!", which considering the size and consistency of his deposit, was actually a very accurate description.

This is when Charlie and I decided to vacate the premises for the relative safety of the back porch, only to find that the hummingbirds had already laid claim to this particular piece of real estate; they say there is no rest for the wicked, I just didn't know that we were this wicked.

Hey, dad…

What's up, Charlie?

It takes a pretty special breed of momma to put up with this circus, doesn't it?

Yes, Charlie, yes it does.

Happy Mother's Day!

Charlie: Anticipation

Yo, dad?

Wassup, Charlie?

Sure is quiet around here with mom and that hairy little goober gone; even Mia is moving a bit slowly since mom took her to get hit with a shovel.

Uh, Charlie, there was no shovel involved; mom took Mia to get "spayed" not "spade" … anyway, this whole bed thing works out a lot better with everyone else gone, don't you think?

Don't get used to it, dad; you do realize that after Thursday, we will both be crammed down inside the same sleeping bag every night?

Yeah, Charlie, about that; I bought you your own ground pad and blanket, but still you persist in wedging yourself into my space, with absolutely no regard for the fact that a Big Agnes sleeping bag was created for one human, not one human and an ox. Besides, aren't you supposed to be a strong, independent, woman, capable of thriving under extreme conditions while traveling through the backcountry?

Uh, dad, I am strong, but I'm also smart; I spend a lot of time watching the Discovery Channel while you're at work. I am fully aware that we travel through areas where bears and mountain lions might not take too kindly to us encroaching into their habitat.

Charles, have you ever considered that you and I crammed into the same sleeping bag is going to appear to any interested grizzly as a big red double meat beefy bean burrito?

Oh, yeah, but I've thought this out; the way I see it, your girly screams will wake me up, and I can make my getaway, or at least make a move for the gun… uh, there WILL be a gun, right, dad?

Oh, yeah; but have you ever considered the fact that you don't have index fingers to pull the trigger? What are you going to do, throw it at them?

Hmmmm… hey, dad? Have you ever considered just hitting the local Motel 6? I've heard that they'll leave the light on for you.

There are no Motel 6's, or any other, where we're going. We'll be just fine, always are; possible snow and frigid temps at altitude in Colorado, high winds in New Mexico, desert heat in Utah and Arizona, what's not to like? Traveling without adversity is just touring. Besides, this time we're doing things a little differently; we're taking the motorcycle, and two wheels make everything an adventure.

Oh, yeah, that's what this girl's talking about! How about we just drop everything and roll out now?

Not so fast, Chuckilicious; gotta pay the bills first, and besides, Special Olympics is coming up, and that cannot be missed.

Oh, OK, but you do realize that the next four days are going to be the longest four days since before God said, "let there be light?"

I get it, Charles, but before you know it, we will be rolling hard, the cold wind from the distant mountains peeling your lips back from your teeth and making your ears POP like velvety black bullwhips.

Oh, dad?

What, girl?

I love a happy ending!

Dad: Travels with Charlie

When Zach and I were first introduced to royalty back in January 2015, we named her Charlie Bravo in honor of the Honda CB motorcycles we were both riding at the time. I had no idea that John Steinbeck had written a book called "Travels with Charley", in which he travelled across America with his standard poodle, camping incognito in a self-contained pickup truck. His goal was to see the America that was changing in the early sixties before she had vanished entirely.

This was already a dream before I read the book, but after my first reading, it served as a catalyst to solidify my worthlessness for normal society. Especially relevant at the half-century mark in my life was the following passage:

"A kind of second childhood falls on so many men. They trade their violence for the promise of a small increase of lifespan. In effect, the head of the house becomes the youngest child. And I have searched myself; I did not want to surrender fierceness for a small gain in yardage. My wife married a man; I saw no reason why she should inherit a baby."

Wow.

So now we ride, but instead of a truck, we choose a motorcycle. Not because of the "cool" factor, but because of the fact that on a motorcycle, you are exposed not only to the elements but to people's perception of your intentions, be they correct or not. Also, by travelling so far from the safety net of home, we remove the possibility of scurrying towards its warm embrace when things turn a little pear shaped.

A trip has a life of its own; many are over long before you return home, while others continue many years after the bike is parked and the gear is stowed. Our small wanderings are all part of a much larger journey called "vacilando", not wandering aimlessly, but no specific destination in mind. Calvinistic society may look at this as laziness, we prefer to look at it as life, and life is what happens when you're making other plans.

When Steinbeck left on his journey, he packed reams of paper, a typewriter, dictionaries, etc, to chronicle his wanderings, but never wrote a single word from the road.

He preferred instead to let the sum of the experiences simmer and mix, the seemingly at-the-time unimportant flavors mingling with the more piquant spices to create a peculiar gumbo. Charlie and I will be brewing our own stew as we get settled in, but until then, the following are a few of the ingredients we jotted down from the trail:

Fatigue creates fear, which makes fools of us all

The rule of three; you can cross the planet with three pairs of underwear and three pairs of socks. Also, both good and not-so-good things always happen in threes.

Don't look so far into the distance that you don't realize what's right in front of you.

You go where you look.

Truck stops should only be visited at night.

It is entirely possible to get so funky on the road that an icy stream and a washcloth feels as good as a spa day at the Waldorf Astoria; or so I've heard.

Everything in perspective; a mountain in Arkansas is a foothill in Colorado, and a national monument in Colorado is just another tall rock in Utah.

Your world contracts to what you can pack into your bike, then expands to where the bike can take you.

"Alone" isn't a synonym for "lonely".

Even though there are many moments on a journey so unpleasant I wish I could snap my fingers and instantly be back home, those moments are always followed be many more moments where I'm later eternally grateful that I couldn't.

Always avoid the crowds, never avoid the people

Young riders pick a destination and go… Old riders pick a direction and go.

All that wander are not lost, all that lean are not off balance.

And God sometimes speaks in the silence that can only exist amidst the sound of the rushing mighty wind; this wind just happens to be inside a helmet.

See you on the road…

Dad and Charlie, June 2017 Gateway, Colorado

Dad: Roll Away the Stone

More than a few years ago, I went through a "spelunking" phase, cave exploring. Most people have misconceptions about caves, that you can just walk around looking at stalactites and stalagmites, and when you get ready to leave, you just casually walk out and resume their normal lives.

In reality, caves are like Charlie's crate; usually very easy to get into, but sometimes very difficult to escape without outside assistance. And have you ever noticed that spelunkers always seem to be wearing helmets? Most would think that this is to protect them from falling rock, but the reality is that a cave is a very static environment, with change, if it does happen, happening very slowly.

The helmets are there to protect the caver's heads when they forget they're in a cave and attempt to stand up; while a cave is not an inherently evil place, it's very nature tends to keep you on your knees. If you forget, an overhead rock will usually remind you.

In Charlie's case, it was not the feces-covered floor, nor the steel bars of the gate, but the roof of her crate that did the most damage. To this day, the only visible reminder of her incarceration are a few white hairs on the arch of her back where the roof had worn through to her spine as she tried to stand and chew her way out through the top of her plastic prison.

Another vital reminder when in a cave is to place markers as you proceed deeper into the labyrinth, as everything looks different coming out than it did going in. In everyday life, these markers are memories of positive experiences; proof that no matter how dark it may be, there were once better times and there will be again; there is always a way out.

Always remember that while the humidity inside a cave is 100%, the average temperature us 57°; as long as you're moving, you're sweating profusely, but as soon as you stop, the cool rock pulls the heat from your body and you begin to chill, and not in a good way. You can only imagine how you begin to smell after this cycle of heating and cooling repeats itself a few times, or so I hear. No matter how fatigued you get, it's usually best to stay moving.

And while the interior of a cave has its own peculiar beauty, the longer you linger, the more you become accustomed to seeing things only in shades of grey and brown. It's not until you spend an extended time underground that you can truly experience how blue the sky can actually be, or how green the hue of even the most common weeds. Then, after a time, the wonder begins to subside, and we once again take for granted the sublime. It's a crying shame that it seems to take such deprivation for us to appreciate the constant beauty that surrounds us, but that is the nature of man… Charlie does NOT seem to have this problem.

Then, after you gain experience, the logical progression is to get involved in SAR, or search and rescue. This is usually a very difficult but rewarding job, as the more you help others escape their own personal caves (and crates), you more you come to understand your own, and tbe tools and techniques necessary for survival. But to assist others, you have to be willing to go into their place of crisis, and will probably get just as filthy and fatigued, but the difference is that you have been there before, and you can show them the way out.

And that's what Charlie's story is all about; the road trips, Special Olympics, and the antics of the inmates are great fun, but the real message is that only by helping others can we ultimately help ourselves.

Charlie: You Have to fill your own bowl…

…before you can pour from it."

I would love to agree with the author of this statement, but then we would both be wrong; if you wait for someone or something else to fill your bowl before you start pouring into other's bowls, there's going to be precious little pouring going on.

History is full of examples of those who appeared to have nothing making a huge difference by unselfishly giving what little they actually have, and guess what? It always seems to be enough, and the giver never seems suffer additional hardship.

Such is life at the Casa; things have a way of "working out". Christians call it the Law of Sowing and Reaping, Buddhists call it Karma, but it all means the same to this dog: to get, you first have to give, and what you give, pawsitive or negative, will return to you tenfold.

That's not to say that I don't occasionally take some time nibble my own butt from time to time, or thrash around on my back for no obvious reason, or race around the yard, fleeing in mock terror from Sandy's pseudo-attacks. Some would add that time spent on dad's motorcycle falls into this category, but the truth of the matter is that I view this not as recreation, but as a mission. If you ever get a chance to see me ride, you will understand; from the second I mount up, my demeanor is all business. My "Chark" changes from one of aimless joy to strident demand; come ON, dad, times a wastin'! We have things to see and people to meet, and miles to go before we sleep!

I'll leave you with this; years ago, when Zach was small, he had a peculiar way of making friends. Rather than approach a group of kids, he would nonchalantly drag out his coolest toys, his new GI Joe set up, whatever, and casually start playing with it. Although seemingly unaware in the interest that he was generating, dad would notice that he seemed to pick a strategic location in full view of the crowd. The other kids would eventually wander over, and friendships were made.

Dad once had an aversion to telling of our adventures, as he was concerned that others might view this sharing as bragging or "showing off". Now we have come to the conclusion that this page is the equivalent of Zach's methods of long ago, we are simply playing with our coolest toys.

Miss Ellie: Midnight on the the FM Dial

On a dark county highway

Out where Chuck and Stevie were found

Out cruising in the Booroo

To see what mischief abounds

Through the clouds of mosquitoes

Obscuring the pale moonlight

Thankfully there are no abandoned dogs

To be found out here tonight!

(Static)

There's a lady who's sure

That the bed is all hers

And she lives is a house called

Del Whackos

When you get there you'll know

As your eardrums will be blown

A cacophony of loud charking

And yapping

(Static)

Charlie…

You don't have to share the bed tonight

Ajax and Mia are with mom on the couch

You don't care if it's wrong or if it's right

Charlie

You don't have to share the bed tonight

Those days are over

Dad sleeping on the floor is such a sight.

(Static)

"And in late breaking news from the Capitol, Republicrats and Demopublicans have agreed to…"

(Very quick static)

If time was controlled with a throttle

I'll tell you just what I would do

I would spend every day

On life's blue highway

And then I would spend it with you

(Static)

Sometimes you can hear them say

Enough to make you hurl

"With a name like Charlie Bravo

Is that a boy or is that a girl?"

You would think the lack of plumbing

Shows I'm a duchess not an earl.

(Radio off)

Hey, dad…

Yo, Charlie?

Can you roll up the window? It's getting a bit chilly tonight…

Charlie: To Rhyme or not to Rhyme?

Dad and I were driving across the Arkansas delta yesterday, seemingly endless miles of rice and soybean fields stretching to the mighty Mississippi to the east. As usual, dad was scanning the stations looking for something "different" when we happened upon a public radio station announcing that due to a guest cancellation, they would be featuring an hour of poetry.

Poetry? Hello! Most of the time, we like a good rhyme, so we set the cruise and settled in.

Evidently, we have a different view of what the word "poetry" means. To our credit, we stuck with it, thinking it HAD to eventually get better, until the station faded into a cloud of distant static. Incidentally, I think the static was actually more uplifting.

I'm not a literary dog, but I thought that poetry was supposed to have a reason to separate it from just a bunch of words strung together without any apparent rhythm, syntax, or (gasp) words that occasionally rhyme?

A more vitriolic, hate-filled, divisive mess I have never heard, left against right, this color versus that color, gender against gender, and the thought occurred to me: what would Maya Angelou think? Or Walt Whitman? Or James Baldwin? Or any other of the titans of their craft that used their gift to enlighten and elevate, not divide and conquer?

So as the highway thrummed beneath the wheels as dad piloted the old Subaru across the muddy Mississippi, I decided to to scratch out my weak response;

We be of one blood, ye and I.

The media is filled each day
Of those who would thrive on strife
I say "why curse the darkness,
When we can light a light?"

No, life is not a Hallmark card
Sometimes troubles come hard and fast
But if our diet consists of the negative
We are what we eat, just trash

Have these that would divide us
experienced nothing precious in life?
To continuously find joy in spewing such hatred
Is a sickness, it's prevalence rife.

It is said that a house divided
Against itself surely will fail
They who anger us ultimately control us
Only we can their efforts derail

So arise and unplug, and have a big mug
Of high octane coffee and go
forth and Chark Diem, way out on a limb
Find a reason to break status quo

We're all on this great trip together
And we're all along for the ride

So move over, dad, there's fun to be had
it's time for the Charlie to drive!

Dad: It always seems like it's too soon until it's too late

Angel, the grand old lady of the inmates at the Casa del Whackos, passed over the bridge tonight.

I find it hard to describe myself as a "pet owner"; how do you "own" a living creature that controls such a large portion of your heart, albeit for a comparatively short span? I do like the title of "dad", as a parent, not an owner, is what you become when you adopt.

Whatever the title, the tasks involved when you accept responsibility for another living being are sometimes daunting and require us to put our own feelings on the back burner and consider what is in the best interest of all others, and sometimes we have to do the hard things.

Today was one of those days.

For the last thirteen years, Angel has been mom's dog, and aptly named, as she could do no wrong. I have no doubt that, at least as far as mom was concerned, her very shadow (Angel's, not mom's) could heal any known disease. Angel was a Finnish Spitz, a notoriously mouthy breed, and she was mouthier than most; I honestly think that she would have argued with a stump. (What was that, mom? "She did argue with a stump; she argued with you!")

As the years passed, Angel began to slow down, as we all do, and we've known for some time that soon that last trip would have to be made. But as any companion of an elderly dog understands, about the time that that you wrap your mind around the inevitable, the dog seems to have a miraculous turnaround, which in turn causes us to torture ourselves with guilt; why were we so hasty?

Then another turn for the worse, followed by a couple of good days, which is the reason for the title of this post: It always seems like it's too soon until it's too late. These words were said to us today by the vet that led Angel to the bridge, and a more peaceful transition I have never seen.

We brought Angel home and mom and I did the next hard thing, a middle-aged couple burying her out back with Stevie, Max, and Bull Taco while the other inmates cavorted in the rays of the setting sun filtering through the leaves of the pecan tree. While this may seem like disrespectful funeral service behavior on the part of Charlie, Sandy, Ajax, and Mia, it was also somehow oddly appropriate, the circle of life and all that, and besides, this IS the Casa del Whackos; what else would you expect?

Dad: Imagine if you will...

The Casa came into being, first by accident as critters in need just kept showing up over the years, then by design as a place to escape the constant barrage of negative energy on the Web. We consider it an inestimable honor when folks drop in to recharge a bit, whether it be from afar via this page or better yet, in person. Everybody needs a break, and although the Casa isn't a special place by material standards, there is a certain "vibe" here, where sometimes, due to certain circumstances in their lives, those who might consider themselves misfits seem to "fit" for a bit.

This holiday weekend was one of those times; an old buddy of mine has recently lost his wife of thirty years to a bitter, prolonged, war with cancer, and decided to come up from the Lone Star State and hang out with some hillbillies for a few days before continuing his journey west.

We were eating breakfast on Independence Day when Sandy came bounding up onto the back porch with a large slobber-covered box turtle in her mouth. We rescued the turtle from what was certain "death from annoyance", as the inmates all act like every turtle they find was created by Pet Smart for their own personal enjoyment, and placed it in a bucket to be granted its own Independence Day later that morning.

Well, it slipped our minds, as seems to happen more and more these days. Later, my friend and I were standing out front checking out the motorcycles and discussing the vagaries of life, and mom was out on the back porch working on Little Tree the clarinet, when she heard a scratching sound. The dogs were all frolicking around the backyard, and she had forgotten the incarcerated turtle in the bucket, so, mom being mom, immediately assumed that something wild had gotten under the porch. She quickly realized the source of the sound and set out to free the turtle.

This is where you visualize: the Casa is close to the end of a dead end street that ends in a slightly(very) swampy area. So, here's mom, in her leopard print pajama bottoms, clarinet in one hand and bucket in the other, procession of goofy dogs trotting dutifully behind, striding purposefully down the street on a mission like some sort of Pied Piper to free the turtle; and we wonder why the neighbors think we're just a bit "teched".

But this is who we are, and this is how we roll; I personally wouldn't have it any other way.

Dad: Somewhere on the Serengeti

The elusive ebony lioness crouches motionless in the tall grass, the only sign of life being the occasional flick of the tail and the dilation of golden pupils as she watches her prey approach.

Today's ritual sacrifice to the goddess of her raw hunger is a tawny antelope, unwittingly approaching her impending doom on gangly legs. A jackal and a desert fox wait in the distance for the outcome of what is sure to be an epic struggle.

The lioness realizes her strength lies not in her speed but in her power and cunning, so her brain is constantly performing complex geometrical equations involving angles and arcs, when suddenly she sees her opportunity and lunges from her hide. The antelope realizes the impending threat and wheels to flee the looming black death, but it's way too late, and the lioness hits her flank like a cannonball, bowling her over and over in preparation of the death strike, or at least a spare. It's the last frame for the antelope, time to return the rented shoes and go home.

Or is it?

What if the antelope wasn't an antelope at all, but another lioness looking for some prey of her own? And the gangling, doofus, approach just a clever ploy to entice her deadly foe away from the remains of her last kill, and the hunter becomes the hunted? And after a prolonged battle that leaves them both gasping, exhausted and defenseless, they discover that the booty for which they had been battling so fiercely had been shanghai'd by the fox and the jackal?

And the merciless circle of life continues amidst the waving tall grass, high on the plains of the Serengeti.

Note to self: I have GOT to get the yard mowed this weekend; it's a jungle out there!

Charlie: Beebe the King

Before there was me, there was another monarch at the Casa, a dog so vast and dark that he was the canine equivalent of the coming solar eclipse. He was one of a litter of twelve pups left when their mother was injured when a tornado hit the town of Beebe, Arkansas.

Although dad didn't know it at the time, there were some world-class breeders of Labrador Retrievers in that area, and he always suspected that Beebe came from one of these blood lines, as his hunting instincts bordered on mystical. He was a legendary dog, with Beebe stories still being told to this day, but there was one area in which he excelled above all others:

Farting.

It all started when Beebe broke his tail as a pup (a long story on its own). The break was high, towards his already massive butt, so mom, doing what mom does, fashioned a splint out of popsicle sticks and electricians tape. In her defense, the idea did work, and his tail wasn't hanging flaccid, but the popsicle sticks were just a little too close to poor old B-dogs pooper, prompting a "poink" with every step .One benefit was that you always knew when Beebe was approaching;

Poink, poink, poink, poink…

Long after the tail healed, his propensity to fumigate the premises continued. I'm pretty sure the whole global warming discussion was started as a result of one of

Beebe's gastric encounters with a can of Alpo; that dog could prompt a county-wide evacuation with no effort whatsoever.

Early one morning, mom, dad, and Beebe where heading towards the fields; the slightest hint of the sun had began to illuminate the eastern horizon. Mom was curled up in the passenger seat fast asleep, somehow immune to the effects of the gallons of cream and sugar with a splash of coffee she had earlier inhaled. Beebe was in his customary place in the backseat with his head on dad's shoulder, ear to ear, to better communicate thoughts directly between the two. It was a peaceful scene, the miles humming beneath the tires, until…

Poink.

Dad is not a good person. As soon as he heard the trumpet of impending doom, he closed the vents and cranked the heater, and they began to baste in Beebe's airborne juices. The result was so awesome that it woke mom from her comatose state.

"WHAT IS THAT SMELL?"

Dad told her that he had been having some electrical problems with the car and was pretty sure there was some rubber insulation burning somewhere in the dash. Mom, doing what mom does, immediately went into Sherlock-mode, sniffing and snuffling around the interior of the car in search of the source, inhaling snootfulls of dogfart, not realizing that the source of this fine bouquet was sitting innocently on his massive haunches, until another:

Poink…

Although it turned out to be a warm Arkansas day in the fields, it was peculiarly chilly in the car on the trip back home to the Casa del Whackos.

Charlie: The Chark Shall Set You Free

Ever have one of "those" days, when you wake up with a sense of foreboding that something's just "not right" before even giving the day a proper chance to establish itself?

This morning was no different than any other day of the week, except Friday, of course; we all know that every Friday is officially recognized as Charlie Bravo Day. Then I realized the problem; instead of looking upward, outward, or inward for inspiration, I instead looked exactly where I shouldn't have.

I checked my social media.

The negativity was enough to gag a maggot; almost every story concerning politics, division, abuse, bullying, strife, and on and on, but the common denominator of them all?

Fear; how am I to encourage others when I start my day with a big bowl of steaming negativity?

When dad and Zach let me out of the crate, they had no choice but to leave me there while they rode the bikes home to get the truck; I had no guarantee that they would or would not return, but I did have hope. I knew that when they came back, they would come back to the last place they had seen me, so in my mind at least, my opened crate no longer represented a prison but a landmark.

Now that I'm queen of the Casa, I can look back and see that the crate is also an analogy of other areas in our lives; substitute my crate with your cubicle at work, with a toxic relationship, with an addiction, a negative body image, or any other example where we decide, consciously or subconsciously, to stay in a situation that it would be infinitely more preferable to leave? Others may see our crates, and we may see others, and wonder, "how do they tolerate living in such confinement?", when neither party realizes that this is our/their reality?

How many times have we heard of someone losing a job or relationship only to find the freedom to explore new opportunities, opportunities that were impossible to to be seen when being viewed from the inside of a crate? And even the worst of habits can be used sometimes for the good; one of dad's predominate vices is procrastination. Recently, he lost a good portion of soft white underbelly (20#, thank you very much) by utilizing this, putting off that trip through the drive through (breakfast burrito with raspberry sweet tea, please) for just a little longer until he realized he wasn't doing it at all (or at least as often).

The same vice can be used when it comes to giving up; when it feels inevitable, just put it off, if even for a minute. A minute will grow into an hour, an hour into a day, a day into a new lifetime. Although I didn't realize it at the time, this is one of the ways I survived my time in the crate, that, and my dogged determination to never give up, no matter how hopeless and claustrophobic things became.

So go forth and Chark this weekend, and stay aware of those crates that others would use to confine you, but more importantly, be ready to act when you can help free someone from theirs.

Dad: Surfing a Wave of Torque

Charlie is still kicking and thrashing in her sleep, no doubt chasing Stevie through her dreams, so I snagged the Samsung S7 Active from her horny paws before she could wake up.

There have been countless inmates pass through the gates of the Casa Del Whackos, but we've never had one that dreams as much as Charlie, but then again, that's a malady I myself am inflicted with, except during my waking hours when I'm supposed to be a productive member of society. If a woman want to really understand how a man thinks on a basic level, she should read a short story by James Thurber called "The Secret Life of Walter Mitty". What goes on in my head is a mix of Mittyism, Calvin and Hobbes, and Don Quixote, all dictated by the what I imagine being the drawl of Mark Twain.

From the very beginning, the dream I had for Charlie and I was to build a sidecar and cross the country telling her story and blogging from the small places on the map. After much time and effort, the rig was finished and looked absolutely fantastic, but was unsuitable for long distance travel.

Plus it didn't lean; and a motorcycle that doesn't lean is like Tarzan without a loincloth, it's just kind of missing something that's vitally important to the story.

So for the last good while, we've ciphered around, trying to find a good compromise between form and function. The Suzuki enduro did a fine job on the last trip out west, but something that fit Her Ladyship's royalty status was still on my radar. When the Honda CB1100 became available and it was actually mom that made the suggestion that we go get it, that cracking sound that you no doubt heard a couple of weeks ago was caused by the air molecules crashing back into the void created be my immediate departure for the dealership.

So last night was the maiden voyage of the new rig; Charlie knew something was up when I rolled the Honda instead of the Suzuki and did not utter the "G" word in vain:

"Go?"

She has learned to control her Chark somewhat when starting on a ride, but last night, all decorum and training, such as she has, was lost in the wind. She would NOT shut her yap until we were mobile, and then it was just like I dreamed it would be when the perfect bike was found; surfing through the curves on a wave of torque, the time spent on the Suzuki learning to ride together translating effortlessly to the more powerful Honda. But the odd thing was that instead of feeling the urge to really twist the wick, it suddenly felt more appropriate to maintain a more "stately" pace.

"What's the hurry?", she whispered; "we have the rest of our lives…"

Charlie: Marco Polo the Horndog

Well, I guess everybody knows it by now; dad's selective social conscience, known as his sucker-bone, has struck again and there is a now a new inmate at the Casa del Whackos. Dad was told that this dog needed a hero, what he wasn't told was that he needed serious psychotherapy (the dog, not dad; wait, that's debatable… scratch that).

Don Marco checked into the Casa a tiny mass of greasy hair and frail bones; we know very little of his previous life at this time, except that a proper diet and social interaction were NOT part of his daily regimen. He was gimping a bit when he first arrived, as he had been recently "fixed", or as dad put it, "delivered two nuggets short of a Happy Meal". Although his papers claim that he weighed four pounds at time of adoption, we dogs all agree that, judging from the size of his, um, "package", he must have weighed at least twice that before his operation. If Don Marcos ever returns to his pre-Casa smuggling lifestyle, he now has the perfect place to stash any contraband, if you know what I'm saying. Mom says he should have been named Slugger, dad opted for Wun Hung Lo.

Anyway, as he is slowly regaining his strength, he has surely recovered his swagger, which is why he is not putting on weight as quickly as we would like. When your outgo exceeds your income, then your upkeep will be your downfall, and the same is true with Don Marcos. Just because they took his bullets doesn't mean that he's done playing with his gun, and any excess caloric intake he may be experiencing is being exceeded ten times over by his "pelvic aerobics".

Ajax was the first partaker of the fruits of the Don's misguided attentions, then Mia; while Ajax looked alarmed and confused at being assaulted by a Tribble, Mia just looked bored, "is that all you got, little man?". It was all fun and games until he turned his attentions towards me; I'm the Queen, and the Queen don't play dat, yo.

So even though his equipment was taken, the attitude is still there, and Marco remains a mincing category 5 hormone hurricane advancing up east coast of the Casa del Whackos. Mandatory evacuations have been ordered in preparation of his making landfall, but nothing is safe from his incessant pummeling. Mom is even trying to design a device to harness the motion of those mighty loins to a generator so that we can use this power for the good and provide electricity to the those less fortunate.

So as the Queen, I've warned him to tone it down a notch, as he's going to hunch himself to death if he's not careful; he has the rest of his life to molest the laundry, stuffed animals, lawn mower tires, barbecue grills, door to door religious proselytizers, etc, but I fear that he is not heeding my advice, as, if anything, his fervor seems to have increased.

Then, as warned, disaster struck.

As dad let me out back to my "business", the pale light of the rising sun was dispersing the wisps of fog only to reveal the form of Don Marco De La Polo laying motionless in the dewy grass. My worst fears were confirmed when I saw, wheeling in the sky above him, a squadron of buzzards in search of a small but easy meal.

As I dad went to get the shovel, I trudged out to pay my last respects to another young life cut short by lust. As I approached, I was shocked to see Don Marco's left eye crack open just a bit, sneaking a peek toward the sky, and the he hissed at me through clenched lips:

"Get back in the house; I think they're getting closer!"

Charlie: Physician, Heel Thyself

The ancient Chinese had a curse, "may you live in interesting times". It's days like these that make me want to retreat into a cocoon of denial, not just away from the evil events, but more importantly, from the evil surmising that inevitably seems to accompany them.

But then I realize that I have a mission to fulfil, and retreating is not an option. My mission? Nothing grandiose, just to show that there is an alternative to the constant barrage of bad news.

Dad once heard a theory that, from the beginning of time, humans were conditioned as a species to only hear as much bad news as they could positively affect; first as nomadic tribes, then as towns, cities, but that was pretty much it.

Now we're hit with wave after wave of depressing news from around the globe, each cycle pounding the rock of our resolve into shifting sand; before we can recover from one, we're hit with the next, until we say "why bother? If I can't fix it all, why fix anything? Why not relax and let the riptide of depression take us where it may?"

Suicide is one of the leading causes of death in the United States, and I would argue that the depression and stress that precedes it is also a contributing factor in a good portion of the others above it. Heart attacks, strokes, Alzheimer's, etc, all exacerbated by stress; why do we have such stress, living as we do in the lap of luxury at this time in history, comparatively speaking?

We feel that we, and consequently our actions, don't matter.

Dad just finished watching a series on the history of Auschwitz, the Nazi death camp where literally millions of Jews, gypsies, Poles and others were put to death in the crematoriums. As opposed to being depressing, what was so impressive and uplifting is that, with death and immeasurable suffering surrounding them daily, the survivors had one thing that sustained them:

They never lost hope.
I would never compare what I experienced during the time in my crate to the suffering experienced in the death camps, but I can relate to the constant feeling of hope; however faint it may have been at certain times, it was always there. If procrastination is ever a good thing, it's when you put off giving up, if for nothing else but for

another minute. That minute can then grow into an hour, into another day, and even into a new lifetime.

So, what is your hope? Mine is the same as yours, to know I've made a difference. That, and that someday dad and I take the Charkstream across the country. Why? Not real sure, unless it's to show that there is a better way, that there is life after the crate. How and when? Haven't the slightest clue, but we can hope, and you can too. But the quickest way to silence that urgent inner voice is to let it be drowned out with the noise of negativism; CNN, CBS, FOX, ABC, PMS, they're not here to help you, they're here to get rich at your expense by multiplying division.

Well, this girl ain't buying, and I'm not letting dad even window shop; our time together is fleeting enough as it is, no time to waste it on someone else telling us we should or should not be afraid of.

Charlie: Head Games

Another uneventful Charlie Bravo Day dawns bright and early at the Casa del Whackos, except this sunrise finds dad and I banished to the spare twin bed in Zach's old room.
It seems that Ajax is an exceptionally vivid dreamer, and evidently had an episode last night where he was proudly claiming property rights to anything in his vicinity by marking his territory, if you know what I'm saying. Unfortunately, dad's physique resembling that of a fire hydrant caused him to be the target of Ajax's fixation, and

the poor guy awoke to find himself being baptized by a sprinkling quickly approaching one of total immersion. It was NOT a joyous conversion; as dad levitated from beneath the covers and Ajax himself was immediately granted the gift of flight, resembling a small hairy Icarus soaring towards the sun, only to find himself, upon landing, facing an extended sentence in solitary confinement. Mom, using her panther-like reflexes, quickly laid claim to the territory of the couch with Mia and Marco, and here we are.

We inmates absolutely LOVE toilet time at the Casa, whether it's our own at 0400, or better yet, dad's, just whenever. The "clunk" of the toilet seat announces to all the dogs that we now have a captive audience, and here we come, stampeding in droves like a bunch of Black Friday shoppers amped up on pumpkin spice latte and greed.

I usually start the assault by bulldozing the phone (or whatever else dad has in his hand) aside in a demand for immediate, undivided attention. This results in dad's voice raising at least two octaves, his gruff demands to be left alone sounding less like that of an irritated dwarf than of a Viennese choir boy. Of course, no one takes him seriously, and his requests for solitude only pour fuel on the fire, as we then know we have him exactly where we want him. We are convinced that Mia has some anteater buried somewhere back in her ancestry, as she has an uncanny ability to apply her whuffling, needle-like nose and darting tongue with alarming precision.

Being the smallest of the inmates, Ajax and Marco have discovered that, behind the toilet is an amazing little tunnel that must be explored again and again. This results in an insane game of "ring around the the rosies" with dad's position on the throne being the center of the ring. The game increases in speed and intensity until soon the scene begins to resemble a solar phenomenon, with Dad being Saturn and the two smaller dogs transforming into the snarling, hairy outer rings.

Then this morning the unthinkable happened; the whirling dervishes achieved such a feverish pace that the they actually wore completely through the tile, eventually cutting a perfect circle down through the sub-flooring that caused dad and the toilet to crash through to the bottom floor, leaving him in a pile of dust and rubble with his pants around his ankles.

Actually, that last part isn't exactly true, as dad isn't high-falutin' enough to afford a two-story house, and the Casa is built humbly on a slab. What is true is that the dogs have actually worn a groove 12" wide and 8" deep directly into the concrete, effectively forming a moat of sorts, albeit without a drawbridge. This is actually not a bad thing, as should the toilet ever spring a leak, we now have a bit of unintended flood insurance, although it does also have its downsides as well; the resulting chasm makes navigation of the bathroom difficult if someone doesn't want to cut the light on.

Just pause and consider that bit of information the next time you feel like complaining about the toilet seat being left up or down, according to your proclivities and/or anatomy.

It's all just a matter of perspective.

Dad: The Owl

Dad here; early Wednesday AM at the Casa finds me wide awake at the results of one of the two greatest alarm clocks ever invented. Nothing will cause human to levitate from an advanced stage of REM like the sound of a dog yarking; thankfully, this was not the case today, just a frantic mass of cold noses and darting tongues. Of course, I'm thinking that they need to be immediately let out lest we are to encounter some mushy little landmines, not realizing that mom had already let them out and they were simply sharing the experience.

The Casa del Whackos is located in a semi-rural area; over the years, we've had visitors such as bats, geese, wood ducks, the occasional snake, and some we know are there but can't always see. Last night mom spotted a two-foot-tall Barn owl perched up in a tree not twenty yards from the back porch, partially illuminated by the backyard street light. Pretty cool, eh?

Well, I know what you're thinking, because I'm thinking it as well; a predator of that size could swoop down out of the darkness and snatch Marco, and possibly even Ajax, so quickly and silently we would never know what happened. So hold that thought, as we'll be coming back around to it.

I recently received word that the son of an old friend had perished this weekend in a motorcycle accident. Although I wish to be very respectful of the feelings of the family, I don't feel that I'm out of line in stating the fact that this person was known to ride "erratically", with no training or safety gear, but sometimes even that doesn't matter.

Ecclesiastes 9:11 states "chance happeneth to all men"; sometimes it's just your time, no matter how carefully you prepare.

Of course, this makes me pause and consider, as not only do I ride, Charlie rides, mom rides, Zach rides, as do many others that I consider family regardless of whose name is listed on their birth certificates: Nathan, Fletch, Craig, David, Kyle, Donna, Jodi, the list goes on. These guys and girls are accomplished riders and safety fanatics, but as I proved by my chance encounter with a stump to the gut leaving me with a ruptured colon, it can happen anywhere and in the blink of an eye.

Which brings me back to the owl; when we take the dogs out to do their "bidness", we have no idea as to what predator may be in the vicinity. Just because we actually saw him for the first time last night doesn't mean he hasn't been perched up in the big oak, observing our every movement through huge golden eyes. Then again, he may not have been within a hundred miles, and any concern and worry would have been a waste of time.

So, in the case of the motorcycle; do I cease to ride? I think that you know the answer to that, as Charlie would mutiny. Or in the case of the owl, do I not let the dogs out at night? If you've ever tried to simultaneously housebreak not one but two scampering little pee factories, you know the answer to that one as well. Fear is interest paid on a loan that's not due; if we learned anything at all from mom's cancer, it's that nothing is ever as bad as worrying about it.

Like everything else in life, all you can do is prepare the best you can and forge ahead with confidence. Although there may be unseen owls lurking overhead, they're not necessarily YOUR owls, and not everything is out to "get you". But when my time does come, is it inevitably will in one form or another, I would hope that my last moments would not be clouded by fear, fear of ridicule, fear of embarrassment, fear that I didn't "do enough", or the greatest human fear, the fear of not having made a difference.

RIP Justin, and DG, may you also find peace in rest.
See you on the road.

Dad: A Day of Remembrance

It's a late Sunday morning at the Casa, and no one shows any inclination towards rising and shining. It has finally turned a bit nipply on Arkansas, just in time for Halloween in a few days.

The Latino culture has a holiday that also falls during this time, Día de los Muertos, or the Day of the Dead. On the surface, the Day of the Dead might appear to mirror Halloween, but the holidays are actually vastly different, with the Latin-American tradition remembering the lives of those who have left us and briefly inviting them back instead of inciting fear. Through this two-day gathering, families celebrate death as a beautiful, joyful, and symbolic event.

My fascination with the holiday began when I discovered an old cemetery on the outskirts of Antonito, Colorado. This was no ordinary cemetery, with the high desert winds whistling through homemade tombstones, some crafted from stone, others simply poured from concrete. But the real difference was that it appeared that there had been party there the night before. Each tombstone was adorned with plates of food, votive candles, bottles of spirits, decorations, evidence of a remembrance of those that had gone before by sharing the things that they loved as if the departed were still here.

Attending one of these celebrations as a respectful observer, if not as an active participant, is waaaay up there on my bucket list.

So, I would like to extend this Día de los Muertos, this time of Remembrance, to those inmates that have went on before. It is said that as long as a man's stories are remembered, he will remain immortal, and the same is true of dogs, at least here at the Casa del Whackos.

First, there was Stevie Mae, the janky-eyed white boxer mix, that at first was so elusive that it took me weeks to actually convince her to come home with me. The post and video of her eventual capture still has the second largest post count of any on this page, exceeded only by the post announcing her surreal passing away at my bedside. If she were here today, and I do believe that in a way she is, she would be sprawled out on Charlie like dots on a domino. Vaya con Dios, Stevie
.
Then there is Max E. Million, the very epitome of loyalty and devotion. He filled a void at one of those rare times

when there were no other "special" dogs at the Casa, and he was special. Max loved nothing better than travel, perched for endless hours on the armrest of my old Impala, where no amount of coercion could unseat him. Believe it or not, his favorite treat was peppermint Tic Tacs; the slightest rattle of the plastic container would cause him to snap to rapt attention. There's something odd about a dog that licks your face with perpetually minty-fresh breath, but that was Max, the Grand Old Man of the Casa.
Angel was mom's dog, and as such, I don't feel qualified to adequately comment on such a regal dog. She has agreed to post her words later in the comments section. I will say that I miss that mouthy old girl.
Then, the one I've been dreading writing about;

Bull.

The story of Bull began on my first day of a new job, when I saw this starving Chihuahua with a broken front leg. Our meeting was in a way symbolic of a new beginning, as I had never wanted to get back into the trucking business, and I also had never wanted a Chihuahua, and on the same day, I got both, and both turned out to be great changes for all at the Casa. Bull was a dichotomy of a dog, self assured but never arrogant, loyal but not clingy, bold but not aggressive; unfortunately, it was his boldness that was his downfall. I would love to find another like him, but I fear that he has no peer, and I would live in perpetual disappointment. Vaya con Dios, El Zurdo.

Charlie: What do you Live For

I live to tell the story
The story of the crate
That no matter where you're trapped in life
It never is too late
Now the ties that used to bind me
Define the task that's been assigned me
Forget the past that's placed behind me
And do the good that I can do.

I live to ride cross country
On the back of dad's black bike
My ramblings? not just physical
Sometimes my words are just alike.
Frequent the hidden places
Seek out forgotten faces
Embrace wide open spaces
Like my words, no end in sight.

I live to make a difference
No matter how odd the way
A dog with pen and parchment
And quite a lot to say
Bards and scribes, poets and sages
Philosophers from all the ages
My words conceived from all their pages
That there is good in every day.

I live to show those damaged
Service to others is its own reward
To ensure their own cup stays filled
They must from it daily pour

Reach out to every stranger
let others worry about the danger
Not a lemming but a changer
Someone's faith in good restored.

I live for those unwanted
Left to wallow in their grime
those told they no longer matter
Cast aside by the hand of time
To learn from past affliction,
Seek out the truth, forsake the fiction
And to form my own conviction
Refuse to feast upon the slime.

I live for those kindred spirits
That share one blood, they and I
Whose actions make all the difference
By their works, He's glorified
The hopeless cause that needs assistance
the awful wrong that needs resistance
For the reward in the distance.
And the good that we can do.

Charlie Bravo
11/5/2017
Chark Diem

Ajax: No Boundaries

Sleeping arrangements have taken a turn for the worse at the Casa del Whackos, at least for dad. Charlie has recently gotten into the habit of beginning the evening by separating herself from the battle that begins nightly at 1030 and retreating to the couch until an armistice is reached. Then, in the wee hours of the morning, she'll decide that she needs some dad lovin's and here she comes, with no respect for any tender vegetation she might be trampling upon.

But the real problem is Marco. When Bull Taco passed while heroically defending the Casa, dad thought he would do a good deed by hosting one of Bull's delinquent, long-haired cousins from south of the border. Little did he know that A, the little varmint would have such Napoleonic tendencies, and B, that mom would fall completely under his Rasputin-like spell. This combination does NOT bode well for dad, as Marco has quickly achieved Finnish Spitz status, and is infallible, at least as far as mom is concerned. When mom gets like this, we all just take a BIG step back; to say that her behavior gets a bit irrational concerning "her" dogs is like saying that Donald Trump is mildly addicted to tweeting and comb-overs.

An example: Mom sometimes has to go in to work early, and even her turning every light on in the house, flushing every toilet multiple times, banging and clattering around the bedroom, all while carrying Marco like some sort of hairy little papoose wasn't enough to roust dad and Charlie from beneath the covers.

Most "normal" wives would come in and say goodbye, have a good day, see you tonight, and so on, but mom doesn't stop there. She flips back the covers just far enough to deposit Marco not just under the quilts, but between dad's legs. The first morning that this occurred, dad wasn't aware that he had been relegated to dog incubator status and awoke later to find that he had apparently given birth during the night to a scruffy little bundle of joy.

Surely, this must have been some sort of immaculate conception, as there were no labor pains, no contractions, no apparent breaking of water other than dad's normal incontinence (just kidding, dad), but here we have a new addition at the Casa.

Some people used to tell their children that babies were delivered by a stork, I think that this one was delivered by a stark, as in a stark-raving lunatic of a dog-loving mom, who would sacrifice her husband's dignity to ensure that her goofy long-haired Chihuahua caught just a few more minutes of slumber under the covers, as this has now become a morning ritual.

Imagine starting the day by lifting the covers to see a smug, tousle-headed, face peering up from the the depths of "down there", looking for all the world like a tawny four pound testicle.

There are obviously no boundaries at the Casa del Whackos.

Charlie: E=MC2

"There are only two ways to live your life. One is as though nothing is a miracle. The other is as though everything is a miracle"

I prefer #2; some may call this defeatist, giving up this much control of one's destiny to a higher power, but I believe there is an order to to the universe, and that nothing "just happens". Every encounter and experience has the potential to be a miracle if we are always prepared to see the miraculous in it, and therein lies our responsibility to recognize and seize the opportunity; service every need as it arises and you will find your ministry.

Consider my time in the crate; regardless of my desire to live, at that time it would appear that I had no control over my own destiny. Sure, initially I railed and tore at the inside of my prison in a frenzy of hunger and claustrophobia, but as my strength faded, it became obvious that my real purpose at that time was what some people might view as lazy or downright surrender; to relax and marshal my remaining reserves of strength.

As a dog, my concept of time is not measured by ticks of a clock; a minute away from dad when he's in the bathroom stretches into an eternity, when eight hours in the car on a road trip to New Mexico passes in the twitch of a tail. As a result, I have no idea how long I was in that crate before the miracle presented itself.

As I heard the motorcycles approach and ultimately stop, I realized that I had been doing my job all along; staying in the game, so to speak, until it was my turn to play. But here is where I gained a new responsibility, to recognize the miracle for what it was and chark the freaking crap out of the diem, not just that day but every day. This is why I sleep harder, bark louder, poop longer, lick lavishly, and most importantly, love excessively. Some may say that I'm not "trained" properly, but I think it's pretty evident by now that some rules don't apply to me, for I am the Charles, and dad and I have an agreement; he does my bidding, and, well, that's pretty much the extent of it. So now I charge and flounce through life, giving freely what I expect to receive as if it is my right, and it is.

But I also have the responsibility to maintain a certain level of situational awareness, to recognize those gifts for what they are; what good is a hundred-dollar bill on the sidewalk if you're so engrossed in your daily drama to even recognize it for what it is? Then again, I also have to be humble enough to accept that gift when it presents itself, as the hand giving is always higher than the hand receiving.

So ultimately both statements are true, only in reverse order; everything is a miracle, a gift, but what good is a gift if you don't open it? And upon opening it, if you don't use it? True, miracles are usually found by looking up, but sometimes found by looking down as well, and you may find that by being someone else's miracle, the life you are saving may be your own.

Oh, and the originator of the opening quote? A man who knew a little something about analytical thinking and miracles: Albert Einstein

Dad: Rollo the Remora

Dad here; this is non-Charlie related, but I humbly asked for and received her permission, so there. I am mortally embarrassed that I have a longtime friend in the hospital dealing the exact same procedure that I had to deal with after my motorcycle accident in 2014 BC (before Charlie), and I am writing this to let her know that it's not the end of the world, although she may think that she can see it from where she's sitting, so here goes...
(Cue the ominous music)

THE COLOSTOMY BAG!!

I typed that in all caps as that's how it registered in my brain the first time I dared sneak a peek under the covers, only to see Rollo the Plastic Remora peeking coyly back at me, securely stuck to my gut although looking a bit deflated. You see, they won't send you home from the hospital until you start "producing", so to speak, and as he and I had just been formerly introduced in the OR the day before, my intestines had not yet received the memo that a detour had been assigned on the roadmap to my bunghole, and went on strike to exhibit their displeasure.

Rollo must have extended an open invitation to all his relatives, as all his little plastic cousins seemed to have set up shop as well. Nora the NG tube snaked her way up my nose and down my gullet, and even I have my limits as to mentioning where the rest of the tubes and wires were inserted and implanted.

I looked like a plumber's worst nightmare.

While I genuinely understand the need for nurses to make rounds every two or four hours to take vitals, etc, I would think, that with all the advances in modern medicine, that the various teams of data collectors would figured out by now how to coordinate their visits to hit at the same time, instead of every fifteen minutes, making it virtually impossible to get any sleep whatsoever; how's THAT for a run-on sentence? It may even be some sort of record.

I was absolutely mis-er-a-ble; I itched like a madman from not being from not being able to move freely in the bed, and finally told the night-time Amazonian charge nurse that I was not a happy camper. Her response: "you haven't had a bath yet? Oh, do I have a remedy for that!"

I immediately stopped itching; NOBODY gives Uncle Bret a bath, especially a total stranger at least double my size, so I declined with thanks. "Oh, you is shy? You gots to be getting over that!", then she proceeded to snatch me out of that bed, stood me up, and before I could even think to protest, had me buck nekkid with my arms out to my sides, plastic tubes hanging everywhere like ornaments festooning an obscene (stumpy)Christmas tree.

She began sanding me down so vigorously that I was sure that she was actually removing layers of hide, using a sponge that to this day I swear had to manufactured out of cat's tongue; she scrubbed parts of me that I don't even scrub. Then she broke out a gallon jug of what appeared to be either horse liniment or Crisco, and proceeded to grease every square inch of me, missing not one nook or cranny. And I didn't care; she was so effective that by the time that she was finished, I felt like an actual human being again, albeit some sort of cyborg, with all the bolt on parts still being attached. I remember telling her "I'm a happily married man, but when I get all these tubes and hoses removed, you and I are going to Vegas!". When Jo Ann showed up at the hospital that morning, I had to make a full confessional as to what had transpired during the night, with the nurse present to verify the accuracy of my story. I have to admit that I was slightly insulted when mom didn't fly into a rage that I had had such an intimate encounter, instead giving the nurse carte blanche to take me wherever I wanted to go, as long as she didn't have to go along as well. As I have mentioned before, I am NOT a good patient.

This is when things began to get better, although the indignities seemed to increase. Walk the halls to get things "working" you say, pushing around what looks to be a transformer pole on wheels? While wearing what is basically equates to a the only garment known to man that makes you feel more naked than if you are actually naked, mincing along like a Japanese tea girl in skid-free socks?

What about the removal of the NG tube, which actually felt like an alien being was being dragged from my chest via my nose? I now understand how King Tut felt when they removed his brains via the same orifice, although he had a distinct advantage over me when he had his procedure performed: he was dead.

So to my friend in the hospital, don't despair. This may seem all consuming right now, but I assure you that you will look back on it and laugh. Get well soon, M.

Dad: The Infamous Poop Story

I was made to promise upon pain of death to include this story should this book ever go into print, so you can blame that person in New Mexico for it's inclusion; proceed at your own risk.

I dug through the archives in search of the original story, but either A: mom destroyed it, or B: it was written before Charlie started the blog, and it was nowhere to be found. Technically, that lets me off of the hook, but I'm a man of my word, so as Doc Holliday said in Tombstone, "I have not yet begun to defile myself"; but I'm fixing to…

Jo Ann tells me that they gave me explicit directions before releasing me from the hospital concerning the care and feeding of Rollo the Plastic Remora, a friendly if somewhat clingy colostomy bag, but I was so far up the river of De Nile that I don't remember a word of it. All I knew is that I was going home with a wound still partially open, a piece of intestine where a piece of intestine should never be, OUTSIDE MY GUTS!!!, and this plastic abomination hanging off my side, allowing me an up close, second look at the biscuit that I had so recently enjoyed.

Mom would come in all chipper from work, and say "how was your day?" "Oh, just heavenly, considering I've been sitting here in this recliner pooping into a Glad Bag all day, but thanks for asking". The one thing that kept me going was the prayer that a pair of Jehovah's Witnesses would show up at my front door one day, and I was going to give them more than one reason to run screaming for their bicycles. And no, you do NOT want to know what I had in mind; some things are much better left unsaid.

My first day home, a shower was in order if for no other reason than to establish some sense of normalcy; well, I soon figured out that THAT train had already left the station. I had been told I could remove Rollo to shower, but they neglected to tell me that I needed to put him back on ASAP. As I hadn't eaten any breakfast, I thought I was safe from any disturbances in the force, or that I would at least receive some warning of an impending movement, and I'm not talking Beethoven's fifth.

This was to be Winingar's Second, if you know what I'm saying.

So there I was, not a stitch of clothes and shaving cream on my face, and I literally heard a tiny "poink". Before I go any further, two things must be made clear. First is the location of the stoma, where Rollo hung out; in my case, it was on my left lower abdomen. The second thing is that in my younger days, I was a very good at footbag, also known as Hackey Sack. So when the "poink" announced the arrival of a tiny turd, old habits die hard and my first response was to catch it on my left foot. Before I could get my mind wrapped around this development, here comes turd number one's twin brother, which I also deftly snag, this time with my right foot.

So now what? Mom's just on the other side of the door in the bedroom, but I'm not about to call her for assistance; who wants their spouse to see them looking like a buck naked Karate Kid with shaving cream on his face with a turd on each foot? And what did I expect her to do except have a heart attack laughing, and I was in no condition to perform CPR? Besides, I quickly realized if there were any future little bundles of joy to be dealt with, I was out of feet and I had to act fast. So I goose stepped like some sort of naked, deranged Nazi stormtrooper over to the toilet and booted the offending articles into the abyss.

I do believe that was the lowest I have ever been in my life; I remember standing there and thinking "it cannot get any worse than this"; of course, this was before I knew about a thing called a barium enema, but that's another story. I swore to myself that I would never speak of this whole sorry affair to anyone, that no one needed to know of my abject humiliation.

Then I thought, "my buddy Marty would crack up if he knew about this", and knew that I just had to tell him. That's when I knew I was doomed, that before it was all said and done, I would be yelling at complete strangers at the mall, "hey, wanna hear a funny poop story?"

Our misfortunes are not our own to hold tight in the darkness; sometimes the only way to get a wound to heal is to rip off the bandage and expose it to the fresh air and sunshine. Then others can learn from our experiences, or in my case, walk away shaking their heads, eternally thankful and thinking,

"At least I don't have HIS problems"

Dad: Today is not That Day

Dad here; I came in from work tonight, tired (but not the good kind) from putting out fires at work; and not even the satisfying type of fires, where you get covered with a manly layer of soot and ashes. No, just the run of the mill type where no actual energy is produced and the only burn involved is to the heart.

So, I came home, let the dogs out to do as much damage as is caninely possible to themselves and others as they stampede around the yard in the darkness. Max and Charlie have found a stick of evidently colossal value, based on the way each is demanding access from the other, and Micro Polo wisely determines that gross tonnage equals right of way and stays outside of the orbits of the other hairy meteors.

After they have worked themselves into an absolute frenzy, then it's time to carry that excitement into the house and deposit it on the living room floor. Micro chooses tootsie roll form, while Charlie goes the polar opposite route, yarking up a biscuit she had snagged off of the kitchen table. Who says we don't know how to have fun at the Casa?

Things finally calmed down for a minute, so I took the opportunity to build a fire for mom to come home to. I then kicked back on the couch and prepared to take an extended trip to Planet Smartphone; this was not to be. Before I could assume a prayerful position with the S7 Active held reverently before my face, a wave of dogflesh engulfed me like a hirsute tidal wave.

As I fought like a madman to escape the snarling mass, I thought of a cartoon I had recently seen: a man and a dog, sitting on a park bench. The man's mind is full of thoughts about material things, planes, cars, money, fame, but the dog's mind is only is full of one thing;

a man and a dog, sitting on a park bench.

Well, f you put it THAT way… I put down the phone, and let the dogs have their way. The way this usually goes down is that Charlie pins my shoulders with her elbows, rendering me incapable of her slathering tongue. Ajax hits whatever Charlie is leaving exposed, waiting for that perfect shot between the lips or up the nostril, and Mia cleans up with her specialty, the ears. Echo is content to keep thrusting her head up under my hand, and I am content with this as well, given her propensity to hurl without a microsecond's warning. Marco prances around on my head, but once again, decides that the odds are against him, size-wise.

Finally, even I have to say "no mas", as I feel like I'm being waterboarded with dog spit. And as I scrape the accumulated spittle from my face, I think that there will someday be a day when I won't be able to enjoy this; someday either I or the dogs will be gone, or greatly diminished. That how differently I might have responded to Stevie, to Max, to Bull, had I known seconds before that that would be the last lick, nuzzle, or bark.

But like those days, I know that someday I'll look back on these days and remember…
But today is not that day.

Dad: Stop, Drop, and Roll

We've all heard the instructions; when you're on fire, stop running, drop to the ground, and roll to put out the flames. Sound advice in the literal, but even more effective when the fire seems to be internal, or "shut up in my bones", as the old prophet said.

There is always so much to be done, and at the very least, work always seems to expand to fill the time allotted. Sometimes you just have to stop running, drop everything, and roll hard out of town, but this time for new horizons. Destination? Not important. Method of transportation? Who cares? Distance? Matters not a whit, as long as we're stepping outside our comfort zone. Sometimes the call to GO is so urgent that even the prospect of sleeping in subfreezing conditions while sharing accommodations with one very inconsiderate dog is infinitely preferable to remaining stationary like a good little boy.

But what is much more terrifying to me is when sometimes we DON'T feel that urge. Life becomes too comfortable, excuses begin to come too easily, and it becomes too easy to say "why?"

I have to say "Why not?"; it seems to me that this is when it's most important to rise and shake myself until my ears pop like Charlie's, dig into my internal (mom would say infernal) file of excuses to GO!!! and do just that.
And "why not"? These were the favorite words of my friend Kevin who passed away a few months ago, and no, the short trip Charlie and I are on is not some maudlin

memory cruise in his honor. It just makes me think of how little time we are allotted, and how sometimes I just have to admit that Charlie is right and I need to relent and say the most beautiful word in the world (to her ears, anyway)

Go?

And right now is one of those times, as writing has became a futile endeavor; even though it's not yet daylight, she is currently engaging in a campaign to get me moving, escalating from intense staring to abrupt nosing, then thrashing about while emitting this incredibly high pitched whine directly into my inner ear in the most annoying manner possible, much like the world's largest hairy mosquito, but without any of the mosquito's redeeming social attributes, as at least a mosquito can't chark.

How's THAT for a run-on sentence, eh?

Dad: The Baconator

Dad here: mom just fried up some maple-flavored crack cocaine, er, bacon, and brought a plate to the bedroom for me to sample. Of course, her approach down the hall was announced by a cacophony of dog hooves clattering on the faux wood flooring, produced by a posse of prancing pups hoping to relieve her of her burden before she ever makes it to her final destination.

I find it odd that the smallest dog is always the one that makes the most racket; Marco's toenail cadence is at least three times that of the other dogs, and his demanding yips and yowls are the most annoying sound of anything this side of a televised political debate, or, dare I say it, The View.

So mom leaves me with two slices of artery-clogging nirvana, and takes the rest of the stash back to the kitchen from whence it came. As I begin to inhale the narcotic aroma in anticipation of indulging in my gluttony, I felt a sudden disturbance in the force; somehow, something just didn't feel "right" about the situation.

Was it my conscience telling me that, yes, I do have an addiction, and should seek intervention?

Then I realized what it was; although mom had left with the full plate, all of the inmates were still hovering around me like a cloud of vultures, eyeing my meager two pieces with looks of total entitlement. That's when it dawned on me; my problem wasn't the addiction, but that I'm an enabler, a total pushover, the new fish walking across the prison yard of life, easy pickings for those whose senses have been honed to recognize and exploit any sign of weakness in others.

In my case, dogs in general, or more specifically, the hardened criminals of the Casa del Whackos.

When did this affliction start? I really can't remember a time that dogs didn't rule my life, and it only seems to get worse as I age. As I drive down the road, I find myself talking to dogs that can't even hear me, dogs in other cars, dogs trotting across fields, whatever; this is usually not a problem as long as I'm alone, but occasionally will have a customer with me who finds it a bit "odd", to say the least.

Unless they themselves happen to be "dog people". I figured out a long time ago that there are three types of people: people who don't like dogs, people who like the idea of having a dog(the vast majority), and dog people. For better or worse, I am a dog people.

There, I admitted it. They say that admission of addiction is the first step towards recovery; I say that they, whoever "they" happen to be, are full of partially digested Gravy Train, at least in this case.

Because this addiction isn't caused by a physical craving(well, it is, but we'll discuss that later) but on love. What but love caused the first wolves, the ancestors of our current masters, to desert their own packs and wild freedom to become the servants of man? And this very completeness of love can also earn him/her the term of deepest contempt, "you dog!"

The least I can do for thousands of years of absolute loyalty is to attempt to return the favor during my short time as the Warden of the Casa del Whackos.
But I'm still not giving up my bacon…

(Charlie here: he's lying like a politician under oath; we got our share of the bacon, don't you worry about that)
Chark Diem!

Dad: Clear Horizons

Dad here; peace reigns supreme in the predawn hours at the Casa, but such wasn't the case just minutes ago. Have you ever seen the movie "Alien", when the crab-like creature wraps itself around its victims face like a mask? Well, that's how Marco decides to wake me up every morning. After cuddling peacefully with mom all night, he wakes up with an overwhelming desire to launch himself onto my face, making my alarm clock consist of gnashing teeth and snarling halitosis.

Of course, this gets the other dogs riled up, but as soon as the maelstrom reaches a fever pitch, they all collapse back into slumber, littering the bed like so many victims of unopened parachute accidents, and leave me wide awake when I would rather be dreaming of clear horizons. Alfred Hitchcock was once asked to define happiness, and that was his answer:

"A clear horizon — nothing to worry about on your plate, only things that are creative and not destructive... I can't bear quarreling, I can't bear feelings between people — I think hatred is wasted energy, and it's all non-productive. I know we're only human, we do go in for these various emotions, call them negative emotions, but when all these are removed and you can look forward and the road is clear ahead, and now you're going to create something — I think that's as happy as I'll ever want to be."

Of course, you know Charlie's response to reading this the first time, and to be honest, mine as well; it's all about the travel. As a matter fact, she never made it farther than the "vast horizons" phrase and she was off on one of her tangents about the next trip, when we're going, how far, etc.

But the line that hit me was "and now the road is clear, and you're going to create something." Not necessarily go somewhere, although around here, that's always a distinct possibility, and for no discernable reason whatsoever, but to create something. Then it dawned on me; at this stage in my life, I can't think of many things that make me happier than creating this blog. If we are traveling, its always with an eye to describing the experiences we encounter. Some can't be described, (at least until the statute of limitations expires), but they all add spice to the gumbo.

Confinement, rather it be physical, mental, or spiritual, self-imposed or enforced by others, is the ultimate definition of hell, as in confinement, you can't visualize that clear horizon.

And without a vision, the people perish
What you can't visualize, you can't create, whether a work of art, the perfect curve on a motorcycle, a particular piece of music, or a release from a restrictive lifestyle; you first have to see yourself as successful.

A quick example; we often go on motorcycle trips with riders of varying experience levels. I have found that a rider that starts at the back of the pack tends to stay there, and even worse, his skill levels tend to diminish as the day progresses and he falls farther and farther from the pack.

But if he/she is ever given the opportunity to feel success, to lead instead of follow, even if for just a bit, his riding smooths out and his skills and confidence seem to magically grow. Then when it once again becomes his turn to follow, he does it willingly, because he was given the chance to visualize the open road before him, and its all about the vision. Or as stated concerning dog sledding across Alaska:

Unless you're the lead dog, the view never changes.

I think often of Charlie's time in the crate, and as horrible as it was, it was no more or less disgusting as the crates we place ourselves in daily. Not just because they prevent us from helping ourselves, but more importantly, they impede us from helping others.

To paraphrase John Milton:
"These crates that would bind and restrict our view,
Tomorrow to fresh woods, and pastures new!"

DAD: THE JUNGLE BOOK

Yesterday I was talking to one of my oldest and wisest friends… I don't mean old, as in "ready for the home and having a problem with incontinence" old, although after some of the barbs she threw my way, I shouldn't feel the responsibility to clear that up. I should let you go on thinking that she is doddering around in a housedress clutching her walker with the tennis balls on the feet because the DMV took her license, leaking a trail of urine to mark her progress around the house, but although I love to talk smack, I have to be honest.

She has a quad cane, not a walker.

She is an incredibly intelligent and well-read person, and it surprised me that she didn't know the origin of the phrase I use all the time, "we be of one blood, ye and I". It is the key phrase in Rudyard Kipling's novel, "The Jungle Book", one of my absolute favorites.

In the book, any animal in distress, no matter carnivore or herbivore, could call out this phrase known as "the word", and the other animals would come to their aid. Even Kaa, the massive snake, and Bagheera, the panther, lived by The Word.

The only animals who didn't abide by the the word were the Bandar-log, the monkey folk; they had no respect for themselves, so how could they be expected to have respect for others?

I would love to tell you how it plays out, but you'll have to read it for yourself. Whatever you do, don't count on Hollywood to tell you the story; those blithering idiots made the book into a blockbuster movie and never once referred to the most important point that Kipling was attempting to convey: that underneath our different hides, were are all connected.

Leaving that key point out of the movie was like leaving the mask off of Zorro, or omitting Tarzan's loincloth; I kept waiting and waiting, even for a mention of The Word as the credits rolled, but nothing, which to he honest, is what I should have expected. Expecting Disney to provide anything of real substance is like expecting 7-11 to provide a nutritious meal, and then blaming them when I overheat my iced honey bun in their crusty microwave and burn the roof of my mouth.

Or so I hear...

Regardless, I was so bummed I almost demanded my money back, but that would have been admitting that I was there in the first place, so I packed up my dismay and stalked out of the theater in a cloud of righteous indignation worthy of the codgiest of old codgers.

So when I use The Word at the end of a post, it's simply to confer that, although our skins colors, nationalities, opinions, religions, etc, may differ, we are all as one; brought together by the unlikely story of a charking dog and crappy crate.

And to my friend? It warms the cockles of my heart to hear of you overcoming your recent adversity, but more importantly, hearing of your happiness. And I'm not even sure what "cockles" are, but they are warm nonetheless.

We be of one blood, ye and I.

ALONE

Dad here; my humble apologies to Cody Jinks, but when his song "Alone" became one of my favorites, it just made sense to apply it to the early morning insanity at the Casa del Whackos.

 Well, it's long before sunrise
The dogs begin to groan
Mom pretends that she's asleep
So down the hallway I must go
Mince along on my bare feet
Through a minefield made of bones
I'm not angry, I just want to be alone

I open the door, the dogs run out
To bark at things unknown
The neighbors ready to strangle me
All hope of peace is gone
There'll be no return to the land of Nod
I'll just play here on my phone
I'm not angry, I just want to be alone

I pour out last night's coffee
I put a fresh pot on
I shuffle back to the bedroom
To find that my warm spot's gone
One dog refused to go outside
I'm guessing Charlie by her yawn
I'm not angry, I just want to be alone

One by one, the dogs come in
They leave me no time to prepare

They leap onto the covers
With no regard what's under there
I've no need for contraception
Our kids have grown and all left home
I'm in agony, and I wanna be alone.

Mom brings me a cup of coffee
Catches me in mid yawn
There's a chihuahua surprise between my thighs
Where he makes himself at home
There's already four, so what's one more
To interrupt my dawn
I'm not angry, I just wanna be alone.

Then, at once my strength renewing,
Though the dogs have crushed me down,
I must burst from 'neath the covers
And defy all their hairy frowns
For the coffee's ran right through me
I rush post haste for the throne
Please forgive me, I just wanna be alone

I don't need Charlie company,
I just wanna be alone.

DAD: LESSONS FROM CHARLIE

Dad here; I've been dreading this post like getting a root canal for some time now. Not because anything bad has happened, but because it involves me coming out of my own crate.

We have all heard the terms "introvert" and "extrovert", but I recently heard the term "ambivert". As I understand it, an ambivert is a person that shows the world the face of an outgoing entertainer, but is also has the tendency to withdraw into the role of an introvert to regain their "mojo".

Sound familiar?

I was recently asked how finding Charlie has changed my life, and it's caused me to think long and hard on how to describe the impact. Apart from the obvious, adopting not just a dog but a force of nature that is as focused and intense as anything I've ever seen, she gave me a voice.

Some would say just the opposite, the I gave her a voice, but they would be incorrect. I have always seemed to have the blessing and the curse of being involved in drastic situations, almost like I go out in search of drama, but that has never been the case; the Bible says "fools rush in where angels dare to tread", and I must lead the league in rushing. Weird experiences just seem to "happen".

Then I turned fifty; things slowed down, and I was struck with the fear that my life of adventure was over, and if there is no hope of adventure, imaginary or otherwise, just roll me into a hole somewhere and start shoveling.

Then my friend Trevor was hit by the drunk driver and I got involved with his cause, and the coincidences and odd experiences started coming so hard and fast that his mother Pam said, "you have to put this in a book". But how? I had never written anything non-work related, and besides, how do you write in the first-person without appearing hopelessly narcissistic?

Then I had the motorcycle accident that almost killed me, and left me for a time with the humility of a colostomy bag as a constant reminder of my own mortality; the first phone call that I remember receiving in the hospital was Pam; "this is your chance to write that book", meaning that I was going to have some recovery time on my hands. Although that was true, I was still stuck with the initial problem: how do you write about your own thoughts and experiences without looking like an ego-ed out middle-aged guy in search of validity?

Then Charlie was placed in my path, and she and I began to find our voice.

Things went well at first, as we determined that the page would be a non-saccharine place on the web to escape the constant barrage of both negativity and the dogmatic foisting of everyone's particular beliefs as theirs was "the only way". The stories were always intentionally light and sometimes snarky, with only occasional mentions of Charlie's original condition to serve as contrast to how far she had progressed, from the Crate to the Queen of the Casa del Whackos.

Then along came Stevie.

Stevie's short time at the Casa was as life-changing as Charlie's, as it was her unusual passing that left me with the immediate conundrum of "how do I put this information out there? This is a place for GOOD news!". On the other hand, the page had progressed to the point that it seemed like we were more of a family by that time than just a random bunch of strangers around the globe reading about the antics of a bunch of hairy misfits from the Deep South.

Writing that post was one of the hardest things I've ever experienced, so far out of my comfort zone that it might as well have been someone else. I was going to have to reveal real feelings, and I couldn't let Charles do the talking, as I'm the dad, and that's what dads sometimes have to do, full disclosure, as uncomfortable as it may be.

So, if you sometimes wonder at the proclivity towards embarrassing tales told here that others might have the wisdom to keep better left unsaid, along with the tragic recounting of such stories involving the passing of Bull and Max, this is why; this is life, and we're all in it together. Although I refuse to sugar coat it, at least we can have some fun with it.

And life with Charlie just keeps getting better, to the point that I almost feel like we're bragging when we post of our adventures; while bragging might be expected behavior from a Queen, it's usually not quite as acceptable coming from the portly driver of the motorcycle. But that is my crate to escape from as well, as although there is a time and a season for self-depreciation and reflection,

The world benefits nothing from you or I being shrinking violets.

So that's how living with Charlie has changed my life, and it can change yours as well. Do you have a gift? Don't discount it, use it to benefit others, no matter how ridiculous or insignificant you may feel it may be. If you feel like doing a little flouncing? Flounce away, regardless of what others might think; those that dance appear insane to those who are deaf to the music.

I consider it one of the greatest experiences of my life that you allow us to be a part of this family of misfits from around the globe, brought together by the improbable story of a goofy dog with a message, that we all have a gift, and we all can make a difference.

We be of one blood, ye and I.

DAD: THIS TOO SHALL PASS

Sometimes, it seems like change comes at you so hard and fast that the passage of events becomes but a blur. On the other hand, it also seems that the more things change, the more they stay the same.

Everything moves in cycles; without valleys, there would be no mountain tops. Without violent stormfronts clawing the debris from the treetops much like a woman clawing at the bedsheets during childbirth, there would be no room for new growth. And that's what it's all about:

Growth.

If you're not green and growing, you're ripe and rotting, but sometimes it's difficult to feel the life inside, buried deep within the heartwood. Have you ever pruned a branch that you were sure was long dead, only to find green signs of life under the rough exterior? And you wished that you had given that particular branch a little closer inspection?

And how long should a negative cycle last? How long should we just "hang on"?
I can't answer that, but I did defer the question to Charlie, who told me:

"As long as you have to; hope never fails if you wait".

And when the "valley" experiences pass, as they always do, why do we spend so much energy while on the mountaintop fretting about the next valley?

I think that this is nowhere more evident than in learning to play music, as the process is very much akin to a personal relationship. A budding musician goes through the initial phase where every note, every chord is a revelation, and they just can't seem to "get enough". I remember mom actually buying me a rocking chair to put out on the front porch just to get me out of the house; I played ALL the time, and loudly.

I was not good, but I thought I was.

Then as I progressed, I began to improve, but soon hit a plateau where no improvement was apparent as it was so incremental. I began to do the worst thing a musician or writer can do, comparing myself with others, and Discouragement moved in along with his deadbeat cousin, Reality.

"He that compares himself with others is not wise" II Cor 10:12

Then other interests crept in as well, and before you know it, that phase of my life had passed; not necessarily the love, but definitely the infatuation. But I knew it was always there, somewhere deep under the surface, waiting to be re-awakened.

When I found the new/old mandolin on the recent trip to Ola to meet Claire the foster dog, it was like finding my first banjo twenty-five years ago; priced WAY beyond one of my rank beginner status, but it didn't matter then, and it didn't matter now; this was the one. It has prompted a spark that has grown into a flame. Do I have any delusions of grandeur, maybe hitting the stage at the Grand Ole Opry with Marty Stuart? Not on your life; this one's all for me.

Just kidding about Marty Stuart; I would be there in a second, even if it was just to have the honor of tuning his guitar.

Mom put out the first hummingbird feeder a couple of weeks ago, and we have been waiting for the first of the feathered welfare recipients to arrive. There had been no sign of the little ingrates until yesterday, when I took the mandolin out on the back porch to make a little racket, and lo and behold, a solo hummingbird appeared. No doubt a scout sent in advance of the hordes poised to the north to descend on the Casa del Whackos.

Call it a sign if you want, I just take it for what it is, a pretty dang cool thing to happen.

So if you're on a seemingly endless plateau, don't walk off of the edge; stay there until that new instrument, that new project, that new direction even, is shown to you.

For good or not so good, this too shall pass.

FOOTPRINTS IN THE CHEESE DIP

Betsy Robb is owed a huge debt of revenge. If you will remember, she's the president of the Friends of the Little Rock Animal Village who originally tuned up and played dad like a Stradivarius. This particular song ended with the relocation of Marco Polo de la Horndog to the Casa del Whackos, and life has never been the same.

Then dad saw on her FB page that the Sonic now has hot pretzels; they'll be good, she said. How could this dose of dough, salt, and cheese dip possibly have a negative effect on dad's diet?

So last night, mom and dad piled in the old Subie to go look at life vests for the canoe; of course, Marco and I had to go, but mom decided(unwisely) to take Mia as well. Mia loves to ride, but unfortunately the motion of any car causes her yarkometer to dial up, and it's never a question of if, just when.

When most folks want to see rednecks go fast and turn left, they watch Nascar; we go to the Sonic, so this is where we stop on the way home from Bass Pro. Car load of dogs, Sonic drive thru, Bass Pro, sounds like some sort of trailer park trifecta. Combine that with the fact that I feel the need to Chark my head off at every carhop that slouches past, Marco bouncing from lap to lap like a caffeinated chigger, and you cannot describe this in any way as a relaxing evening.

Dad spots the pretzel with cheese on the menu and is immediately reminded of Betsy's post. In addition to that, many drive thru items are decided based on their ease of being shared with we dogs, the true rulers of the Casa.

The prolonged preparation time more appropriate for a five star restaurant than a drive through gives Mia's stomach plenty of time to attain trebuchet status, and she launches her projectile just as our dinner is being delivered. Mom may be unwise, but she is always prepared, and has a towel in reserve for such an attack. If course, dad's thoughts on the matter run more towards "if you're so sure she is going to do the Technicolor yawn, why bring her in the first place?"

So, dad divides the pretzel, and begins to part our half with all the care of Jesus feeding the multitude with the loaves and fishes. Marco is in full prance mode in dad's lap, demanding his share and mine as well, and dad is just about to enjoy his half of the pretzel when he makes a horrifying discovery:

Marco has trodden in the cheese dip, leaving a perfect Chihuahua hoof print.

To be totally honest, dad's first instinct was to quickly smooth it over, pretend it didn't happen, and eat it anyway, but believe it or not, even he has his limits.

Thanks, Betsy, and I mean it.

(Kind of)

AJAX: DAD'SGONE!!

OMIDOGOMIDOGOMIDOG!!CLAIRECOMEQUICKTHISISTERRIBLEOHNOWHATAREWEGONNADO?

whuuuut?

MOMJUSTLETUSINFROMOUTSIDEANDDADSGONEOMIGODWHATTAWEGONNADOWHATIFHEGOTCAUGHTUPINTHERUPTURE?

whuuut? Charlie's in there on the bed where dad usually is, why don't you go ask her?

OMIGODTHAT'STRUEMAYBESHEATEHIMNOWHE'SALLGONEANDWE'REALLALONEWITHMOMANDSHELIKESMARCOBESTANYWAYNOWHE'LLGETALLTHEGOODSNACKS!!!WHATTAWEGONNADO?

Ajax! Chill out already! Do you need to go find some of Bull Taco's hidden stash to calm your nerves? I'm sure that Charlie didn't eat dad, and if she did, we need to go check it out; he had him some nice stocky legs, so I'm sure she left some bones to gnaw on… why don't we go ask her?

THAT'SRIGHTWEHAVETOFINDWHATSLEFTOFHIMBEFOREMIADOES! SHEDOESN'TSHAREWELLWITHOTHERS!

(Scamperscamperscamper)

CHARLIEWHERE'SDADWETHINKHE'SGONEFOREVERDIDYOUEATHIMIFYOUDIDTHAT'SCOOLIGUESSBUTWHERE'STHEBONES?

Ajax, you spaz; he's not gone, he's just in the bathroom. I'm keeping his spot warm until he gets back. Have you been digging in the trash again? Maybe found some coffee grounds? You're WAY too jacked up for a Saturday morning.

OMIDOGTHEREHEISWETHOUGHTYOUWEREGONEANDMAYBECHARLIEHADEATENYOUANDCLAIREWANTEDTOCOMEFINDYOURLEGBONESTOCHEWONBUTIDIDN'T WELLIKINDADIDBUTNOTREALLY!

(Dad) sometimes I wish I were a cat person.

Book V: The Road Home

DESERT SOLITUDE

"The role of the artist is not to tell people what to think but rather to encourage them to think for themselves."

Charlie here; things have been so loco around the Casa del Whackos that it has crowded the ability to chronicle those changes. Dad's dad is rapidly declining , (uh, I'll be having the Parkinson Special with a side of Alzheimer's, hold the shake), and the sight sometimes takes a bit of the zip out of our doo dah.

But it also reinforces my appreciation for Charke diem-ing, if you will, living in the moment; every day out of the crate is a good day. The following words were written in the early 1600's:

Gather ye rosebuds while ye may,
Old time is still a-flying;
And this same flower that smiles today
Tomorrow will be dying.

It also gives me a new appreciation for the loneliness of both the sufferers of
mental illness and that of their caregivers, as the patient gradually retreats into the shadows of their mind, and the other feels that life is marching on without them while they, alone, wait on the inevitable.

I recently read a study that stated the physical effects of chronic loneliness was equal to that of smoking a pack of cigarettes a day; dad says both pale in comparison to watching even fifteen minutes of the news, but I digress. Loneliness is very much like depression as the sufferer can sometimes help heal themselves, as reaching out to others is the most effective cure for what ails ya.

But my time in the crate taught me many things, not the least of which is that our own conditions can severely hamper our own efforts to reach out to others, but that doesn't mean we should stop trying. Dad still has my former crate, and the claw and bite marks on the inside bear mute witness to my determination to not be forgotten.

But solitude is not necessarily loneliness, for it's in those times that the greatest growth occurs. If loneliness is the state of being acutely aware of your aloneness, then solitude is different: to be solitary is to be inside yourself with no need for escape- a separateness without the human ache of isolation.

Sometimes I think that's why dad and I live to travel by motorcycle; no cell phones, no media invading our world and sucking at our souls, but always knowing that we have the option of making a human connection at almost any stop we make.

But therein lies the secret: we have to be willing to stop, and most of the time be the party to initiate contact. That's why travelling alone on the road is rarely lonely, and always a party; people can't come in unless you unlock the door, but sometimes you at least need to turn on the porch light and let them know your available for visitation.

Dad has a few adventures of his own on the horizon, one that he is taking with others, and one he is going alone. The first is the scary prospect of ACTUALLY FINISHING THE BOOK! The final 10% of any project is the most difficult and the most important; the writing is finished and, for the most part, very close to hitting the presses. Stay tuned for updates.

The other is that dad is taking Jehu the mighty Suzuki back to Moab in a week, going with Zach, Craig, and Levi; I'm sitting this one out as the trails he will be taking under the blinding Utah sun are not conducive to black dogs on bikes. He may even find a way to sneak down into New Mexico and pay a visit to the sisters of Our Lady of the Desert Monastery, maybe uncover a little more info on their meeting with Trevor all these years ago.

So, we have a lot of preparation over the next week, but that won't slow us down; Marty Stuart is in town Saturday night, so you can add that to the list of activities as well....

It's always a party at the Casa, and as always,

Happy Charlie Bravo Day!

REMEMBER YOUR FATHER AS HE WAS...

...not as the man he is today.

It's been a rough week at the Casa, with dad spending too many late nights at the VA hospital dealing with the effects of dementia. I know what you're thinking, that if we're just now figuring out that dad doesn't just have issues but has a lifetime subscription, we're a bit late to the game, but this time I'm talking about his dad. Dementia and Altzhiemers are terrible conditions to have to deal with at the end of someone's journey, as it's hard not to let the most current uncomfortable memories obscure a lifetime of achievements.

So what do we do when you get a break from the insanity? Well, I don't know about you, but we go for a ride. Dad and I let the motorcycles rest for a morning and took Miss Ellie the Ancient One for a little jaunt. One area where the old Subaru is lacking is her sound system, er, radio. While there is something endearing about the old buttons that you have to pull out then push in to preset what few stations you can pull from the sky, it limits the choices, to say the least.

As usual, the Saturday morning airwaves were polluted with self-righteous financial planners whose message is A, how much money do you have for retirement?, and B, which overpass have you chosen as your future residence in which to spend your golden years?

Whether its politics, religion, or financial planning, we've learned long ago to distrust anyone who touts an issue that only they can solve. As dad's idea of planning for the future is leaving wadded up dollar bills in his pant's pockets to be rediscovered later in a celebration of new found wealth, this cacophony of faceless, staticky voices only serves to remind him of his many inadequacies, so we do what we do best:

Turn them off.

Denial is much more than just a river in Egypt, and one that we seem to spend a lot of time navigating it's muddy waters. Then I think about those lying in convalescent homes, more than willing, even desperate, to exchange their entire bank accounts for a little more time, or at least an unsolicited touch from another living being. I don't care how much money you make, if your last shirt has pockets, take all you can take; we all go out with nothing, just like we came in.

Although the beginning and the end of any journey seems to get all the press, we know it's what we do during those sometimes seemingly insignificant highway miles between the two that matter the most. When it's all said and done, what defines us is not our jobs during that time or the manner of our passing that defines us, but how much we were willing to do for others.

The secret of happiness doesn't lie in religious doctrines, political platforms, or any other agenda that serves to separate and not unify; The secret seems to lie in unselfish service to others. Before Jesus preached a single sermon, His years were spent healing the sick, comforting the feeble minded (there IS hope for dad!), touching the untouchables. It was only then that His previous actions caused people to receive his message.

Well, dad and I don't aspire to be any sort of diety, but we can charge through what's left of our time, not in pursuit of adventure, but always in search of the next cause, be it tiny or humongous, were we can make a difference.

And that's what "Chark diem" is all about, as everyday outside of the crate is a good day.

Vaya con Dios…

> **Non nobis solum nati sumus.**
> (Not for ourselves alone are we born.)
> ~Marcus Tillius Cicero

DAD: THE ROAD NOT TAKEN

"Two roads diverged in a yellow wood,
And sorry I could not travel both
And be one traveler, long I stood
And looked down one as far as I could"

I awoke before sunrise gasping for air, my gills flexing for oxygen like a fish out of water; what was this devilry all about? How could it be possible to be having a panic attack while camping somewhere as invigorating as the Rocky Mountains?

True, I knew this trip had the potential to be stressful, considering my dad's condition back home; it seems nothing will make you selfishly consider your own mortality like a major life change in the life of a parent. Then there was the situation involving my friend Craig's motorcycle accident in Moab, but he HAD ridden it out over twenty-five miles of inhospitable terrain, so it was obvious that, with that type of intestinal fortitude at his disposal, I needn't concern myself with that, so what could so the source of my anxiety be?

Then I remembered: I WAS camping at 11,000 feet, and oxygen is a limited commodity at this altitude, so I rolled out of my blanket, scrubbed my face with some snow left over from last winter, and here we are.

How often do we enhance the drama occurring in our own heads with that of the circumstances that surround us, usually well out of our control?

Thunder heavy rain
Thin line between joy and pain
It's a long strange trip it's all insane
You ain't never gonna be the same
 -Cody Jinks

So now I begin my descent from the mountains towards an unclear future; like most people since the beginning of time, I have always looked for signs and guidance from others to show me direction, disregarding the series of wonderful miracles that have brought me to where I am today. If God Himself choose to grace us with an incredible vision of some sort, laying everything out before us in vivid Technicolor, how are we to ever trust in the very Faith that we have planted in us in the first place?

Though I am thankful for the pastors, shamans, parents, physical angels of every cloth that are put here to guide us, ultimately, we alone are responsible for time spent on this earth. I came into this world naked and screaming, or so I hear, and I genuinely hope to leave it the same manner; it's what we do in between that matters.

At well past the half century mark, it would be easy to consider that I'm way past my prime, and that my best years are behind me, but I'm just getting started. I do know that the Bible does NOT say "the greatest in the kingdom is he that sitteth through the longest sermons", or "he that hath the largest bank account", or even "he that is capable of kissing the most hind ends", but it does say "the greatest in the kingdom shall be the servant of all". Everyone has their own calling, and if yours is different than mine, that doesn't make it wrong. All I know is that before Jesus ever attempted His first sermon, he had spent years feeding and tending to the baser needs of others; I think that sometimes we get that whole process a bit backwards from His example.

"I shall be telling this with a sigh
Somewhere ages and ages hence:
Two roads diverged in a wood, and I—
I took the one less traveled by,
And that has made all the difference."

See you on the road…

Manga Pass, Colorado

PINON NUT FUDGE BROWNIES

Dad has finally made it back home to the Casa, a fact that we inmates have milked to the Nth degree. I let the mom think that she ran things with a much firmer hand in his absence, but now that the little pushover is back, we have retaken command of the bed and she has retreated with her disciples Marco and Mia to lands unknown; it is rumoured that she has (gasp!) gone as far away as the Land of the Couch!

Dad and I have had an opportunity to talk a bit about the trip, and an eventful trip it was to say the least. But with any journey, adversity, and how and when to deal with it, are an essential part; adventure without adversity is just touring.

The second day of the journey found dad in his happiest of places, north and west of Taos along the Rio Grande. The funkiness and openness of the New Mexicans contrasts with the sometimes brutal landscape; this is when you you know that, regardless of which direction of the compass you are following that this is "way out west".

There's nowhere else like it.

Though not really physically hungry, Dad decided to stop in Tres Piedras to grab a bite; between you and I, I think he could go a week without eating out there, but don't expect him to go fifteen minutes before attempting some human interaction.

So, like some sort of unholy combination of Tyrion Lanister and The High Plains Drifter, he waddled purposefully into the saloon, er, diner, on the edge of the dessert. After bellying up to the bar, he directed his steely gaze towards the menu only to discover the Holy Grail of snack foods:

Pinon Nut Fudge Brownies.

He wasn't even sure what "Pinon nuts" were, but it surely didn't matter; the lure of the unknown combined with the siren call of the familiar made the decision an easy one, and he decided to make his play for the heavenly brown squares in the basket on the bar.

Not so fast there, pardner; there were some new desperados in town, a pair of posturing pistoleros from somewhere back east: Lycra Larry and the Spandex Kid. They had already eaten and were waiting to pay for their hardtack and jerky, so dad, (graciously, he thought) allowed them to proceed before placing his own order. This is when the Spray-tan Kid noticed the brownies in the basket and GRABBED BOTH OF THEM.

This would not do; the Low Plains Midget confronted the dastardly duo concerning their lack of dessert decorum, and the bar became silent as the combatants faced off in what would surely be spoken of in years to come as the Gunfight at the "Not OK with It" corral. Dad's hand swept for his weapon, only to realize that:

He had left me at home; served him right, or in this case, he didn't get served at all, as the rude nincompoops refused to relinquish even one brownie, and he had to hang his head and slouch sheepishly from the scene without the provisions that would have surely allowed him to survive the remainder of his trip across the dessert.

I know what you're thinking; why didn't he just snatch one of the brownies from her callused claws and make a dash for the hills? Well, obviously, you haven't seen dad lately; the only dashing he does these days is done from the back of a motorcycle. Dashing is not in his repertoire; waddling, maybe, sauntering, most definitely, sometimes even a short scamper is in order, but never dashing. He even has had to give up wearing cowboy boots due to his (lack of) stature:

The shanks kept rubbing calluses on his butt cheeks; now I defy you to shake THAT image from your mind without using peyote or prescription pharmaceuticals.

As he continued west, he began to dwell on the encounter with the carpetbaggers, to the point that it began to tear at his guts like a buzzard sitting on road kill. Then he realized that he ran the risk of ruining the rest of the day, and possibly the trip, if he continued to fixate on the bad instead of concentrating on the good and forging ahead.

But wait; why so quick to forget the "bad" experiences in the first place? Why not first embrace them, squeezing them ever tighter until every drop of hidden goodness is extracted from the pulpy mess? Only then could he really leave the bitterness in his rear-view mirrors to decay and become just another pile of bleached brownies decorating the dessert landscape.

Let the buzzards continue to wheel and circle above the piles of offal you leave in your wake as you travel forward; we have miles to go before we sleep.

See you on the trail.

DAD: THE WAITING IS THE HARDEST PART

My dad has begun his final retreat, this time to somewhere deep within himself.

In the beginning of the process some years ago, it was a bit hard not to be resentful; after all, how could he NOT remember who I am? I, who for years was the most important thing in his universe? And how is it fair, just when I think that that we have finished raising our own children, somewhere along the way we have acquired another, albeit without the hope of a storybook ending?

Then, after years of slow decline hastened by a perceived lack of respect and an abundance of stress, his condition took a sudden steep nosedive, and he became increasingly difficult to manage. One extremely horrible Friday night, we had no choice but to take him to that most dreaded of health care facilities, (cue ominous music here),

THE VA HOSPITAL!!!

Don't ask me how I was aware, but I did know in the pit of my gut, that he would never come home. But I did relearn a valuable lesson: don't let other's opinions form my own. I had heard all the self-righteous radio talk shows castigating the VA system, and I'm sure that there is some truth to that side of the story, but I'm here to tell you that I cannot say enough good about the quality of care, both physical and mental, that we have received.

And the people; I cannot imagine working in a health care environment where death is so often the expected outcome, whether due to the age or the social status of the average patient that enters that system. It is beyond my comprehension how these angels keep plugging tirelessly away; forget the stars of Hollywood and the sports world, these are the true heroes in my book.

So after many weeks of fighting the good fight, the adversary eventually has proved to be too relentless and a cessation in hostilities has been declared. For everything there is a season, a time to fight, but sometimes a time to realize that one has fought the good fight and kept the faith, and now it's time to surrender and let someone else carry the banner.

So now he's been moved into palliative care, and the final withdrawal from the battlefield has begun. Is it sad? I'm not so sure, as I know the respect and honor he has waiting for him on the other side, as he sure didn't get it here.

I recently read an analogy where death was compared to a dog waiting for her dad at a closed door to another room. Even though she had no idea what else was on the other side of that door, it didn't matter; what did matter is that was where the dad was at, so it HAD to be good, and that's where she wanted to be.

Of course, I had to laugh when I read this as it pertains to Charlie, as if there is any chance of the Charles waiting at any door without A: tearing it off of it hinges, or B: charking her goofy head off until she eventually gets her way. I pity the eardrums of St Peter and/or the conditions of the Pearly Gates should she be denied access; when the roll is called up yonder, she'll be there, or wherever she decides she wants to be, that much is for certain.

So, I leave town this morning on a business trip, not knowing if I will even make it to my destination before getting called home because my dad did. On the other hand, it may be weeks or more; who knows? It's out of my control;

Sometimes all we can do is wait.

THE END OF AN ERA

It has been a while since a true "Sunday post" here at the Casa del Whackos; life has been coming so hard and fast that it has been difficult to back up and process the insanity.

We had some visitors from up north yesterday who did us the inestimable honor of sacrificing their vacation to come meet Charlie; of course, the Charles found nothing odd about this in the least, as everyone that shows up at the Casa is here for to pay homage, as far as she is concerned. This is not just visitors, but myself and mom as well; I swear that she is such a diva that you would think that it was Beyonce herself who goes scooting across my threadbare carpet, not some refugee from a stinking crate.

Since the death of my dad, there has been very little weeping and wailing and gnashing of teeth, but trust me, the void is still there. It seems that we're trudging through cold molasses, everything taking a bit more effort than it used to: this is a bit odd, as he had been sidelined long before being removed permanently from the game. Nothing has really changed, but then again, everything has.

The end of an era seems to be a bad thing, but the end of one always seems to make way for the beginning of another. But the scary thing is:

"What's next?" And the answer is always the same, "who really knows?"

We were talking with our visitors yesterday about the burden that some of us seem to place on ourselves; animal rescue, people rescue, being a chauffeur to a diva of a dog, sometimes the demands come so hard and fast that we feel overwhelmed. This is compounded by the fact that people with our calling often have to do the hard things, sometimes being forced to take actions that would appear heartless to the uninitiated, so we labor alone. Sometimes all you can do is the best you can do for as long as you can do it, then lay awake at night trying to figure out how to do more.

So, then the stress begins to build, and we start thinking that it might be time to withdraw a bit; you know, recharge the batteries, get a fresh start, maybe back up a little and let someone else carry the torch, right?

Hogwash.

We all think that, but what happens when we get that reprieve, and things seem to go smoothly for a while? I don't know about you, but I start feeling pretty dang useless. And how far do you back up before you have found that you have in fact backed out, rejoining the multitudes of mindless automatons marching lockstep to the cadence set by those who would have us believe that our actions don't matter?

Service every need as it arises and you will find your ministry; yours, not someone else's. Just because your calling may be different than mine does not make it any less vital, and vice versa. If all the crayons in the box were the same color, the resulting picture would be pretty nondescript and boring.

But some of us take the concept a step farther, forsaking the prescribed boundaries set by the creator of a particular coloring book in favor of the uncharted territory offered by a blank canvas. To be able to imagine a finished product where some see only emptiness is a great gift in and of itself, regardless of whether the project actually bears fruit.

So, don't quit; as it just so happened on that cold, dreary, day in January when we first spotted the Queen's crate:

The life you save may be your own.

My Father's Son

My history is no secret, my failures are well known

Brought up to trust and depend on God but tried to make it on my own

Due to choices that I made, I bear the scars of sin

I cast aside my birthright, the son of righteous men

Raised to be among the few, I chafed at the demands

Passed my youth between these pews where I grew to understand

Sacrifices made before had smoothed the path for me

I owe to those who follow, to live accordingly

Young men have the vision, old men dream the dreams

Those that labor for the truth will pass from the scene

If that cup should pass to me, to do what must be done

When they lay me down remind them, I was just my father's son

He worked among the people, heard their testimonies told

Delved into sacred teachings, like nuggets of pure gold

As his strength began to fail him, his faith showed him the way

That by God's grace he'd be right there, on that final judgment day

We are given comfort, facing Jordan's rising tide

No battle's every hopeless, if we'll lay down our pride

Will my boy learn from me, stand fast instead of run

Will he like me be blessed to see he's still his father's son.

The young men have the vision, the old men dream the dreams

Those that labor for those less fortunate will pass from the scene

If that cup should pass to him, to do what must be done

When they lay me down remind him, he's just his father's son.

Charlie: In pursuit of Happiness

It's almost impossible to believe that it has been almost three years since I exited my crate and took my place as the Queen of the Casa del Whackos. I have settled into a comfortable place in my life, but I fear comfort as much as I fear discomfort, for it is in times of stress that have also been my greatest times of growth.

Only in moments of extreme fatigue do I catch a glimpse of that ragged scarecrow of a dog, but at the same time, it's also getting more difficult to see that idealistic young dog with the insane drive to "DO SOMETHING!, anything, to make amends for time wasted in the crate.

As I approach middle age (for a dog), I find that happiness is not an object to be pursued like a stick thrown by dad, always in a mad rush to ensure that Ajax doesn't get to it first. Neither is happiness a feeling to be found on top of the mountains and hoarded against the day it might not be so easily found while in the valley.

Maybe the purpose in life is to not strive to be happy at all. Just maybe, it is to be useful, to always be available, to be honorable, to be compassionate, to have it make some difference that you have lived and lived well. What if in only in the service to others can true happiness be found? I hope you'll remember Jesus on the hillside, feeding the multitude; not because He was seeking influence and not because it was in His job description—but because they were hungry and He wasn't okay with that.

Zig Ziglar once said, "you can have everything you want in life, if you first make sure that others get what they want", but I think that it all comes down to what motivates you; would you rather make an impact or an income?
I want to make an impact.

And the time is now. My whole life has somehow pointed me towards this moment. I found the following passage, author unknown, on dad's phone this morning:
"Our deepest fear is not that we are inadequate. Our deepest fear is that we are powerful beyond measure. It is our light, not our darkness, that frightens us most. We ask ourselves, 'Who am I to be brilliant, gorgeous, talented, and famous?' Actually, who are you not to be? You are a child of God. Your playing small does not serve the world. There is nothing enlightened about shrinking so that people won't feel insecure around you".

Now is my time, as it is yours, to arise and shake myself; on one paw, today's date is just another day on the calendar, but on the other, every day, every minute, for that matter, is a new chance to restoke that fire. Live every moment for others, service every need as it arises, and you will find your ministry.

And your happiness;

And they all said…

CHARK DIEM!

Made in the USA
Lexington, KY
05 August 2018